*Holding the Lotus to the Rock*

# Holding the Lotus to the Rock

## THE AUTOBIOGRAPHY OF SOKEI-AN,
## AMERICA'S FIRST ZEN MASTER

### Edited by Michael Hotz

*Four Walls Eight Windows*
NEW YORK

© 2002 The First Zen Institute of America

Published in the United States by:
Four Walls Eight Windows
39 West 14th Street, room 503
New York, N.Y., 10011

Visit our website at http://www.4w8w.com

First printing April 2003.

Library of Congress Cataloging-in-Publication Data:

Sasaki, Shigetsu, 1882–1945
    Holding the lotus to the rock : the autobiography of Sokei-an, America's first Zen master / edited by Michael Hotz.
    p.    cm.
    ISBN 1-56858-248-x (hardcover)
    1. Sasaki, Shigetsu, 1882–1945. 2. Priests, Zen—Japan—Biography. 3. Priests, Zen—United States—Biography. I. Title: Autobiography of Sokei-an, America's first Zen master. II. Hotz, Michael. III. Title.
BQ984.A676 A3 2003
294.3'927'092—dc21                   2002153080

Design by Terry Bain

All photos ©2003 and courtesy of The First Zen Institute of America.

10 9 8 7 6 5 4 3 2 1

Printed in the United States.

# Contents

# Introduction

*"I brought Buddhism to America. It has no value here now, but America will slowly realize its value and say that Buddhism gives us something that we can certainly use as a base or a foundation for our mind. This effort is like holding a lotus to a rock and hoping it will take root."*

—Sokei-an

Sokei-an Sasaki was the first Zen master to reside permanently in America. He came to this country as a young Zen student in 1906. He completed his training as a Rinzai Zen master, founded The First Zen Institute of America, and died in New York in May 1945. This was all I knew about Sokei-an when, twenty years later, I came to live at his Zen Institute. I found this "Zen" he had rooted in the rock of Manhattan made manifest in the persona of his student Mary Farkas, the Institute's secretary and editor of *Zen Notes*. Farkas spent years collating the notes of Sokei-an's students. As these talks on the classic texts of Chinese Zen were read in the meditation hall, I would begin to smile. This is a funny guy, a born writer, I thought to myself. Sokei-an's talks sparkled with his love of storytelling. For those who found their way to West 70th Street in the 1930s, Sokei-an demonstrated his Zen in silence. When he began his commentaries and translations, he spontaneously acted out all the parts, throwing himself into the roles completely. His childhood in Meiji Japan, wanderings in the Wild West, and struggles during the Depression to teach Americans Zen somehow mingled seamlessly with Buddhism and eccentric tales of Chinese Zen masters. Speaking with compassion and ironic humor about his own struggles with self-awakening, Sokei-an made a gate in your heart and drew you into his experience of Zen.

I enjoyed watching Farkas discover more lost pieces of Sokei-an's "lives" for her articles in *Zen Notes*—his years as a troubled young artist and Zen student after the death of his father; his immigration to America with his Zen master Sokatsu; life as a family man living with Native Americans in the Northwest; his days as a *Dharma* bum and then poet, sculptor, and journalist in the emerging bohemian world of World War I–era Greenwich Village; Sokei-an's transformation into a Rinzai Zen master and teacher; and the details of his arrest by the FBI, subsequent internment at Ellis Island, and death during World War II. Farkas also researched and wrote extensively about the pioneering efforts of Zen masters Soyen Shaku and Sokatsu Shaku, Zen teacher Nyogen Senzaki and Zen scholar D.T. Suzuki. In the 1950s and early 1960s, the story of the early history of Zen in America existed only in *Zen Notes* and Sokei-an's *Cat's Yawn*. Mary Farkas continued to collect letters, art, photos, and memories of everyone who had known Sokei-an. They were added to the vast archives collected in the 1930s and 40s by Sokei-an's Zen student Edna Kenton—an authority on Henry James, a biographer, and the Institute historian.

Some years ago I began looking at this seventy-year effort to preserve the carefully collected legacy of an artist and writer's life. There were sculptures, photos, oil paintings, hand-carved stamps and dragons. There also remained shelves of his newspaper columns, volumes of satirical sketches on American life, and letters in Japanese. On fragile yellowing paper, dozens of volumes of Sokei-an's unpublished talks, reminiscences, anecdotes, tea notes, copies of *The Little Review*, and temple histories were preserved. Also, documents, letters, Shinto stories, fairy tales, short stories, and poems were found in English. Sokei-an, it turns out, was far more than a Zen missionary. In the same period in which he received his Zen master's credentials (1928), he published, in Japanese, books on America with titles like *From the Land Troubled by Women* and *Thoughts on the Red-Light District*. This Zen master I had never met found a place in my heart. I was charmed to find that he was a bit of a character. That familiar smile I get when I spend time with Sokei-an's writings convinced me to organize an autobiography before it slipped away forever.

The decision to edit an autobiography rather than write a biography arose naturally from a desire to preserve Sokei-an's distinctive intimate "voice." The editing process resembled a giant puzzle. It took four years, and the pieces, which often covered every available surface, danced around and then intuitively found their way to tell the story. To help the reader navigate the flow of the text, I organized the selected excerpts chronologically. Originally, I separated each excerpt, but editors and readers found it difficult to follow. Excerpts now run together to create a more seamless narrative; therefore their order does not completely represent the original context. I corrected Sokei-an's grammar, unless it interfered with the flavor or humor of his spoken words. I sometimes combined two versions of the same story to add details.

Unless accompanied by a Japanese title, all of these excerpts, including letters and creative writings, were written or spoken in English. Sokei-an's students also painstakingly recorded and collated Zen commentaries on his translations. I included a bibliography of his extensive translations into English of Buddhist texts, his commentaries, and also one of Sokei-an's literary works. The only pieces still missing from this puzzle are Sokei-an's untranslated Japanese letters, essays, poems, and hundreds of newspaper columns. The Japanese works, translated by Peter Haskel, always appear with their Japanese titles. Sokei-an's creative works in English were placed into the autobiography in rough chronological order to add poignancy to a particular moment. Many Buddhist parables, Zen stories, poems, tales of old Japan, and Sokei-an's own anecdotes of turn- of-the-century San Francisco, the American West, pre-World War I Greenwich Village, and New York during the 1920s and 30s appear in this book.

In the context of twentieth-century history, Sokei-an's life personified the sweeping changes that brought East and West into intimate contact. The transformation of old Japan by Western ideas and power during the Meiji Period (1868-1912) shaped Sokei-an's childhood and led him to America. The decision to make his life in America as a writer and Zen master was the great adventure of his life, but it was also a way to bring something of value from the East to the West. His turbulent immigrant experience included racial discrimination, the Depression, World War II, internment, and death in a country at war with Japan. It is curious how the relations between America and Japan transformed the two nations and Sokei-an's own life. Besides being a chronicle of this meeting of East and West,

Sokei-an's autobiography is also American literature, an account of Asian-American immigrant history, and a portrait of an artist and Zen master.

I tried to find a graceful way to help the interested reader with aspects of Sokei-an's life not included in his own account, without breaking the concentrated flow of the mind of a Zen Master. With this flow as a priority, I finally chose not to use footnotes or include introductions at the beginning of each chapter. Instead, there is enough biographical material here in the introduction to fill the critical gaps and put Sokei-an's life in perspective. The reader can also refer to the source materials provided at the end to enjoy the mysteries and contradictions from the memories of those who knew him, or simply proceed from the introduction and meet Sokei-an "eye-to-eye, soul-to-soul."

Sokei-an was born Yeita Sasaki in 1882. He was later known by his Buddhist name Shigetsu ("finger pointing at the moon") and ultimately by his Zen master name Sokei-an, given to him upon the completion of his Zen training. By his own description, he was a somewhat spoiled, willful, and nervous child. His father, Tsunamichi Sasaki, was a deeply religious man, a priest, and a master of languages. Tsunamichi's wife, Kitako Kubota, was childless. Tsunamichi took a sixteen-year-old daughter of a tea master, Chiyo, as a concubine, who gave birth to Sokei-an. Kitako left the household for the duration of this arrangement. Two years after Sokei-an's birth, Kitako then returned to raise this only child. Chiyo received a dowry, went on to marry twice, and became a successful singer and dancer. Although his stepmother was loving and kind, perhaps the loss of his biological mother inspired Sokei-an's restless heart and deep inquiry into the nature of things.

Sokei-an's father moved several times and held positions teaching Shinto priests languages at Sendai, the conservative cultural center for northeastern Japan. When Sokei-an was eight, Tsunamichi became the chief priest of Omiya Shinto shrine. Sendai still used much of the etiquette and language of the Tokugawa period (1600–1868). Sokei-an's father, an expert on ancient Japanese and Chinese, taught him languages from an early age, and he grew up hearing Shinto stories and fairy tales. Sokei-an recounts many tales of traditional rural Japan and the dramatic intrusion of Western power and ideas that transformed the country in the Meiji era. These changes altered the life of the Sasaki family. During Meiji, when the samurai class was disbanded, each family was given government bonds according to rank. The new government established a religious affairs department that employed Japanese classical scholars and Shinto priests like Tsunamichi to lecture. When it was disbanded, Tsunamichi moved to a village shrine at Goi (Chiba prefecture). It was near Sokei-an's aunt's farm by a small river. Sokei-an had an adventurous boyhood, catching shrimp and absorbing the mysteries of Shinto shrines, Christian missionaries, and Zen monks.

When Sokei-an was fifteen, his father died. The Kubota clan reclaimed Sokei-an's stepmother and dissolved the Sasaki family. Now at the bottom of the Kubota clan, Sokei-an apprenticed with an engraver of Buddhist altars and temple furniture in Tokyo. For one year, he went on a walking tour of the mountain temples repairing dragons and other temple carvings. He then spent two years woodcarving in a factory in Yokohama, where he lived with his widowed mother, then returned to

Tokyo to work for admission into the Imperial Academy of Art. In 1898, Sokei-an became a student of the sculptor Takamura Koun (1852–1934) and gave himself over utterly to art. During this time he reportedly had a very touching and romantic meeting with his biological mother, who was an actress in Tokyo. He saw her for the first time when he was living with his father's wife in Tokyo. She was beautiful and young. He met her in Ueno Park, where they were bothered by the police who thought she was a prostitute that had accosted him. This story is included in his book *Jonan bunka no kuni kara* ("From a Land Troubled by Women"). According to the story, Chiyo identified him by the scar on his throat from a tracheotomy performed when he had diphtheria as a child.

Sokei-an's mother's sister was a geisha mistress in Osaka. Through her he became acquainted with the geisha world and its specialized lingo. Another sister was a *joruri* performer. Joruri performers sing long poems accompanied by a *samisen* as well as puppets in *Bunraku*. According to Mary Farkas, Sokei-an studied with such performances. He wanted to go into vaudeville where his aunt and uncle were appearing.

Sokei-an tormented himself with introspective questioning, and his stepmother feared he would go mad. Sokei-an felt he could not live honestly without some real foundation for his life, and so he began his Zen training in 1901 at a Zen institute for laymen, studying with Zen master Sokatsu Shaku (1870-1954). This Zen group, Ryomokyo-kai, was founded by the reform-minded Rinzai Zen master Imakita Kosen (1812-1892). During the shifting political and intellectual tides of the Meiji era, Buddhism, in a state of corruption, fell into deep disfavor and experienced outright persecution. Kosen had the task of overseeing religious teachings for the new education ministry. He reorganized the Rinzai sect of Zen and became abbot of the Zen monastery Engakuji. Kosen opened Engakuji to lay people, many of whom were university students. He recognized the need to revitalize Zen so it would be compatible with modern ideas and attract educated people. Kosen seemed to take a keen interest in the promulgation of Zen among laymen as well as the lay education of monks. Kosen sent his most brilliant student, the Zen master Soyen Shaku (1870–1919), to a university.

The modern ideas of Kosen and Soyen, the most famous Zen masters of their day, influenced the Zen offered to the West in the beginning of the twentieth century. The first Zen master to visit the West, Soyen Shaku visited America in 1897 and returned in 1905 to San Francisco to teach Mrs. Alexander Russell, the first American Zen student, and her family Zen. With Soyen at this time were two of his students who were also to play a vital role in the introduction of Zen to America, D.T. Suzuki and Nyogen Senzaki. Among those who came to study under Kosen was the young Sokatsu, and after Kosen passed away, Sokatsu finished his Zen study under Soyen Shaku. Soyen gave Sokatsu the task of reviving Kosen's Zen Institute idea. Sokatsu gathered a group of lay Zen students composed of women as well as men at Ryomokyo-kai for Zen training. As Sokei-an said in *Cat's Yawn*, "The formation of this group was of great importance to my own life."

The sculptor Koun and the Zen master Sokatsu became pivotal influences in Sokei-an's life, helping to steady Sokei-an during the extended crisis he experienced after the death of his father. It is interesting to note that this rebellious young art student, whose head was buzzing with Western philosophical ideas, the son of a Shinto priest, turned to the ancient tradition of Zen, albeit the reform-minded Ryomokyo-kai.

Sokei-an had his first experience of Zen answering the *koan*: "Before your father and mother, what was your original nature?" Part of this breakthrough came after he read a translated verse from Emerson and found a new perspective. Then later, cold and tired after walking around a pond near the meditation hall for the third time, he entered the experience of Zen. Sokei-an demonstrated his answer before his teacher and added, "As a man digs and finds wet sand."

In 1905, Sokei-an graduated from the Imperial Academy of Art, and the army immediately drafted him to fight in China. He spent two months in Manchuria driving a dynamite wagon. The war ended and he went home. At this time, Sokatsu introduced Sokei-an to Zen and then invited him on the greatest adventure of his life—to join fourteen other Ryomokyo-kai students dedicated to bringing Zen to America. Sokei-an accepted Sokatsu's invitation. Before their departure Sokei-an married a member of this group, Tome Sasaki, a student at Tokyo Women's College. Sokatsu arranged the marriage. Without a doubt, the tiny, aggressive, and attractive Tomeko also attracted Sokei-an. She was apparently a good Zen student, and her family had money from their seaweed business. It was also to some extent a marriage of expediency.

This group of fourteen, led by Soyen's Dharma heir Sokatsu and Zuigan Goto, arrived in America in 1906, just after the Great Earthquake in San Francisco. They created the first American Zen community, raising strawberries on a farm in Hayward, just outside San Francisco. Educated as university students, they failed as farmers. Sokei-an fought with Sokatsu over this fiasco, and Sokei-an entered the California Institute of Art to study painting under Richard Partington. Abandoning the idea of establishing a Zen community at Heyward, Sokatsu Shaku opened a new Zen center in Sutter Street and later moved to Geary Street.

Sokei-an and Nyogen Senzaki met in the period after the Great Earthquake in 1906. Senzaki did not complete his training with Soyen, whom he revered. He scorned the Japanese religious establishment and persevered in bringing Zen to America. Senzaki and Sokei-an bonded, showing the same courage in facing immigration, internment, and teaching "noisy Americans." Sokei-an and Senzaki were actually more like older brother and younger brother, with all the normal competitiveness, and they could tell each other off whenever either's egotism needed to be addressed. Sokei-an criticized Senzaki for giving koans when he knew better. Senzaki, an orphan, looked out for Sokei-an's son when he returned to the West Coast in 1929. Samuel Lewis, who knew both men, said their relationship was something beyond his understanding, likening them to two tomcats staring at each other across the continent.

In 1908, Soyen called Sokatsu back to Japan for six months. Sokei-an resumed his study of Zen and remained in the U.S. His only son, Shintaro, was born in San Francisco. Sokei-an described the discrimination he experienced in San Francisco. He was not allowed to become an American citizen under then-existing laws, although he held a permanent U.S. visa from 1906 to 1945.

All of Sokatsu's group except Sokei-an returned to Japan in 1910. Electing to stay in America, Sokei-an walked across the Shasta mountains in the snow into Oregon and worked for a farmer dynamiting tree stumps. He went to Medford and then

Seattle, where he reunited with his wife and son. Before the family settled in Seattle, they lived in a shack on an island inhabited only by Native Americans. Tome gave birth to a daughter, Seiko. Tome was happy with life on the island, but was unhappy with the rest of America. Sokei-an continued with his Zen training, delving into the layers of his mind to prove the truth of Buddha's discoveries. He took walking trips through Oregon, Washington, and Montana, and got subscriptions for the Japanese-language *Great Northern News* by promising to write up subscribers' stories in the newspaper. He continued woodcarving and sent back to a friend in Japan a book of stories published under the title, *A Vagabond in America*. During the years that followed, he contributed prose poems, short stories, and essays to the paper under the general title of "Nonsense Sketches."

Tome, pregnant with her second daughter, Shihoko, did not want her last child born in America. She returned to Japan with the children to care for Sokei-an's stepmother, Kitako, who was getting older and wanted her daughter-in-law to come back to Japan to care for her in her old age. Kitako inherited some means from her husband and helped support Tome and the children. Tome never returned to America and eventually entered a mental sanitarium for three years. She became a Seventh Day Adventist. Sokei-an remained in America, but left Seattle. He said he saw his children behind every bush and found it unbearable.

After Sokei-an's family returned to Japan, something in the landscape and in the American experience, for all its difficulties, continued to resonate with him. After wandering the American West, Sokei-an settled into Greenwich Village in 1916. Journalism and poetry replaced sculpture as a priority for him. As he struggled to support himself repairing antiques, he began writing poems, sketches, and fairy tales in English and Japanese. This was the beginning of the bohemian Village, and living in a Washington Square rooming house, he made translations of the Chinese poet Li Po for issues of the *The Little Review*. He published books of poetry, including *Kyoshu* (Homesickness, 1918) and eventually wrote for the fashionable Japanese magazine of his day, *Chuokoron*, and for Japanese-American newspapers. He also published six books of essays during the 1920s on the peculiarities of American life and relations between men and women.

What we know of Sokei-an's Greenwich Village days comes from Mary Farkas's correspondence with the petite and reportedly beautiful Elizabeth Sharp, an old girlfriend of his. She stated that Sokei-an was a colorful figure, probably unrecognizable to those who knew him only as the more mature Zen teacher of later years. He wrote poetry and began writing in English. Sharp wrote how "At a tea he could endlessly recite his own poems. He was slender, somewhat taller than the average Japanese. He looked about twelve or fifteen years younger than his age. He was not without guile. All the women talked very freely and easily to him, as to a precocious youth."

Writing about America was popular in Japan. As an immigrant, Sokei-an observed his surroundings and the American character, and mined ironic humor from cross-cultural interchange. He later used humor and English vernacular expressions to teach Americans Zen. In his Japanese writings, he used American idioms, particularly New York slang, expressing himself in a peculiarly abbreviated and abrupt manner, perhaps also the result of his study of Chinese Zen literature. He also included many allusions current in traditional Japanese literature, developing a style entirely his own.

One very hot summer in 1919, Sokei-an had a second great Zen experience. "I saw a dead horse lying on the pavement in Sixth Avenue. Saw the physical details. Something happened. In that moment, nothing was left in my mind." He returned to Japan in 1920 to finish his formal study of Zen. Sokatsu agreed to the validity of his experience and gave him the seal (*inka*) indicating completion of the formal aspect of Zen training. In 1922, after returning to New York, Sokei-an drifted in what he always referred to later as a state of "false emptiness."

Sokei-an had a semi-permanent visa for the U.S. that became invalid if he remained out of the country more than two years. On October 27, 1926, he sailed again for Japan. He had a third great experience and wrote his teacher, who replied: "You have attained *Prajna* (wisdom) but your *Samadhi* (absorption) is not quite real." "I went back seven thousand miles," Sokei-an wrote. Sokatsu acknowledged Sokei-an's attainment and made him a Zen master, one of only four out of thousands of Sokatsu's Zen students. In July 1928, Sokatsu gave Sokei-an his permission to teach. As a sign of the transmission, he gave Sokei-an a fan used by Soyen Shaku. His teacher gave him the teaching name Sokei-an because "Sokei" refers to the Sixth Patriarch of Chinese Zen, a favorite of Sokei-an's.

When Sokei-an asked his teacher for the money to get back to New York, Sokatsu replied, "There is no such question in the history of Zen." Sokei-an worked in a factory for eight months for the fare and returned to New York. According to Elizabeth Sharp, when he returned to America, he had changed. He appeared much older, and all of his talent and experience became focused on Zen. Throughout the 1930s Sokei-an continued his creative writing, journalism, painting, and carving and casting figurative sculptures. Sokei-an was a dynamic creative personality, but the Zen Master, teacher, and translator began to dominate.

Sokei-an began teaching Zen by giving talks in Central Park and lectures at Orientalia Bookstore. Finally, after some discouraging false starts, he found real ground on West 70th Street. Sokei-an began giving *sanzen* (a private interview where students answer problems that require them to break into Zen and demonstrate it freely) to Americans and speaking of Buddhism and Zen training from the perspective of a mature Zen master. Sokei-an and his students incorporated their American branch of Ryomokyo-kai as a religious organization in 1931. He began translating what he felt were important source materials for American Zen. In introducing Zen, Sokei-an covered an amazing amount of ground, providing Americans with original source materials translated and commented on by an enlightened Zen master. Sokei-an translated from Chinese the teachings of the Zen masters Hui-neng (*Platform Sutra of the Sixth Patriarch*) and Lin Chi (*The Record of Rinzai*). He also translated and lectured on *The Sutra of Perfect Awakening*; outlines of Mahayana Buddhism and Buddhist terms; *Twenty-five Zen koans*; *I Ching*; and the *Agamas*. The variety of Sokei-an translations and commentaries was an accomplishment that can be admired today, but from the perspective of the 1930s, when little of the sort was available to Americans, it was astonishing.

Sokei-an's training as a journalist and Zen master merged as he observed his own heart in the world around him. Sokei-an's familiarity with both Eastern and Western traditions and ways of thinking contributed to the cultural perspective and humor that animated his lectures and creative writing. He could speak about Kant, Christianity, or *Alice in Wonderland*. This unusual combination enabled him to introduce Americans to something as utterly unfamiliar and difficult to grasp as Zen. Sokei-an's commentaries interweave with his own ironic humor and experience of America, and he continued to write poems, short stories, fairy tales, and essays until his internment during World War II. Sokei-an was a dazzling storyteller, and these stories were spoken spontaneously, even acted out before the astonished eyes of those Zen students who found their way to Sokei-an's apartment on West 70th Street in the 1930s. Best of all, Sokei-an always spoke from his own authentic experience and his struggle to penetrate Zen. For all his translations and commentaries, Sokei-an repeatedly pointed out that Zen cannot be taught. The Zen master demonstrates it in his ordinary daily behavior, and the student must break in to share the Zen occasion. The student either catches on or doesn't.

As a Zen master in America, Sokei-an had little success in getting Westerners to practice the formal sitting meditation that had been a part of his own training. His students meditated in chairs before lectures and in preparation for sanzen. Sokei-an had to formally accept students in order for them to take sanzen and was quite strict about its importance. Koan books of students remain in the Institute's archives, signed by Sokei-an. Some of Sokei-an's students like George Fowler, Edna Kenton, and Mary Farkas answered up to seventy koans. Those who have studied Zen will understand this was a considerable achievement in the 1930s.

Ruth Fuller Everett, wife of a successful Chicago attorney, was introduced to Sokei-an by Dwight Goddard in 1933. She became a student of Sokei-an's in 1938, remarking of Sokei-an's presence in sanzen, "You had a feeling this was not a man, but an absolute principal you were up against." Everett, who eventually married Sokei-an just before his death in 1945, had

*Sokei-an, Ruth Sasaki, her daughter and Alan Watts. Sokei-an is wearing a fake mustache and hat for a masquerade benefit party.*

previous experience with Zen in Japan with the famous Zen master Nanshiken at Nanzenji. Alan Watts, Everett's son-in-law and author of many books introducing Zen to Americans, did not last three weeks in sanzen with Sokei-an. Watts observed that Sokei-an always moved slowly and easily, with relaxed but complete attention to whatever was going on. He described Everett as "something of a social climber." She was keenly interested in "orthodox" Rinzai Zen traditions. Watts said she often apologized for Sokei-an's direct and occasionally ribald expressions of Zen or for his insistence that Zen has no purpose. "Sokei-an was as humorously earthy as he was spiritually awakened," Watts recalled. He said that Sokei-an told him, "if he had any ideal at all, it was just to be a complete human being."

Mary Finley, later to become Mary Farkas, also came to 70th Street in 1938. She was not particularly interested in Buddhism. She decided, however, if what Sokei-an had was Zen, then she was intrigued. Farkas recalled: "In the first degree with Sokei-an you could get into it, and get into it for a long time. It was like standing next to a big gong and feeling its vibration go all through you. Every night Sokei-an would come in, and he would immediately present himself to us. We would be there, and if we were with it, he would be there, too. . . . The particular wave that carried me out to sea was one of millions that pulsed out of his mind, and like all waves extended to infinity as he addressed his audience, his gray cat named Chaka, and the invisible horde of future beings."

As the war approached, Sokei-an seemed to feel the weight of the coming ordeal, and his health began to fail. After Pearl Harbor, the Institute, now in Everett's townhouse on East 65th Street, temporarily closed to the public. The FBI investigated Sokei-an and Everett. On June 15, 1942, Sokei-an was arrested and taken to Ellis Island. "My heart is bruised," he wrote in a letter. Sokei-an and Nyogen Senzaki both were interned during the war, but both remained certain Zen would root and send forth a bud. Just before his arrest by the FBI and internment at Ellis Island, Sokei-an observed, "You say, when I die nothing is left. All becomes nothing. There is neither *karma* nor reincarnation. My individual life comes to an end with death. This is a one-sided view. In the world of desire your desire remains. I wanted Zen Buddhism to be transmitted to America. This desire remains after my death. . . . Every footstep is kept in the invisible world."

As internment took a toll on his health, Sokei-an's friends and students began an intense lobbying effort to get him released. In October 1942, he was sent to Fort Meade, near Baltimore, and on August 15, 1943, Sokei-an's students succeeded in having him released after he was transferred to Fort Howard. Back in New York, after a six-hour hearing at the U.S. Attorney's office, he was permitted to remain on the East Coast. Immediately afterwards, he suffered a coronary thrombosis and possibly a slight stroke. Until the end of March 1944, Sokei-an remained in his room on 65th Street, giving sanzen every day.

In July 1944, Everett and Sokei-an left New York quietly for Little Rock, Arkansas to obtain a divorce from Tome so they could marry, an arrangement that could offer Sokei-an some protection during the war. He was visited by his daughter, Seiko, who had returned to the U.S. in 1930 to look after her brother, Shintaro. Both Shintaro and Seiko had also been interned, and they had all kept in touch. On the train to Chicago, Sokei-an was stricken with a heart attack. Returning to New York, he gave sanzen in his study, mostly from his couch, and continued his second translation and commentary on *The Record of Rinzai*. In the fall of 1944, he said changing the Institute's name from the Buddhist Society to The First Zen Institute of America was his original dream. "If you will do this, I will die the happiest man in the world." On May 12, he was diagnosed with a hemorrhage of the kidneys. Sokei-an gave his last talk and died Wednesday evening, May 16, 1945.

Looking at this historical record, I would say that the introduction of Zen to America is now a piece of the quilt that is American history. I call Sokei-an America's first Zen master. Soyen Shaku and one of his heirs, Sokei-an's teacher Sokatsu Shaku, both came to America and were Zen masters, but soon returned to Japan. The Zen teacher Nyogen Senzaki and the scholar D.T.

Suzuki both studied with Soyen and were great teachers and life-long contributors to American Zen, but they were not Zen masters. For this reason, I call Sokei-an an American Zen master. To my mind, both Sokei-an and Senzaki were true Americans who immigrated to this country as young men, stayed all their lives, and made a substantial contribution. Sokei-an was the first Zen master to permanently make his home in America and the first Zen master to write, translate, lecture, and give sanzen to Americans entirely in English. In spite of the fact that they were not allowed to become citizens and were unjustly imprisoned, Sokei-an and Senzaki also found the freedom in America to simply be themselves and saw this country as a place where Zen Buddhism could take hold and grow. For Zen Buddhists this transmission of the Dharma is part of a much larger 2,500-year-old historical record.

Soyen, Sokatsu, Sokei-an, Senzaki, and D.T. Suzuki were reformers trying to bring something of value to the West: Zen stripped of the superstition and corruption of the religious establishment. These descendants of Kosen, who first brought Zen to America, were bringing the Buddha's experience of awakening as a foundation. The Buddha simply proved that the illuminating principle of being aware from moment to moment is a way through which human beings can unfetter their minds. These reformers felt this experience must transcend national and cultural characteristics and the problems associated with religious institutions.

Sokei-an often spoke about the death of his old teacher and how hard it was for those whose training is interrupted. His early death in 1945 left Ruth Sasaki and Mary Farkas to play a vital role in preserving the introduction of Zen to America after the difficult war years. Although Sokei-an had no particular notion of founding a permanent institution, the Institute's senior members persevered through the most difficult period for Zen in America. The Institute's members continued to meet regularly to practice, holding longer meditation events called *sesshin* and providing the public with information on Zen. The First Zen Institute of America published issues of Sokei-an's newsletter, *Cat's Yawn*, as a book in 1949.

By the mid-1950s, Ruth Sasaki was in Japan to find a new teacher for the Institute. She became involved with creating The First Zen Institute of America in Japan, Ryosen-an, on the grounds of Daitokuji. She assembled leading American and Japanese scholars of Zen to work at The First Zen Institute of America in Japan, continuing the Institute's tradition of preparing original Zen texts in English as a foundation for Zen students. These efforts resulted in the publication of *The Development of Chinese Zen*, *The Zen Koan*, *Zen Dust*, *The Layman Pang*, and *The Record of Lin Chi*.

Mary Farkas became editor of *Zen Notes* in the 1950s, publishing Sokei-an's lectures and telling the story of Zen in America. The Institute moved to her townhouse on Waverly Place in Greenwich Village to meet the new wave of interest in Zen. In 1955, Ruth Sasaki returned from Japan with Isshu Miura, a very traditional Rinzai Zen master she hoped would take over as teacher at the Institute. In 1963, Mary Farkas, Ruth Sasaki, and other senior members bought our current building at 113 East 30th Street. They also devised a plan to make the Institute financially self-reliant. Miura didn't stay, but the plan and the building did work out. As Sokei-an said: "We must wait for the time to come. When the time does come, then a little ant will come and raise the stone. It will be so simple. You will realize then." Sokei-an's dream is still holding a lotus in the midst of busy Manhattan, and Mary Farkas turned out to be the ant who raised the stone. Sokei-an would perhaps be surprised at the hundreds of Zen centers that have sprung up across America through the efforts of a second and third generation of Zen masters and teachers and the hard work of American Zen students.

Few people today recognize how many Americans Mary Farkas helped introduce to Zen at the Institute from 1945 until her own death in 1992. She took sanzen with four Zen masters—Sokei-an, Zuigan Goto, Isshu Miura, and Joshu Sasaki—but had no interest in being either a Zen master or priest. Mary was simply herself. She preserved Sokei-an's work, greeted each new generation of Zen teachers, and told their stories in *Zen Notes*. She always invited people who came to the Institute to enter Zen immediately, and what I remember most was her laserlike Zen eye and silently beamed-forth invitation to play in this living Zen. The thing she loved most about Sokei-an was his lively insistence on manifesting your original nature by responding to the flow of circumstance with a clear, penetrating eye and unfettered spontaneity.

Sokei-an was a creative personality. His recorded poems, short stories, fairy tales, carvings, and paintings reveal a romantic, humorous man who bore his difficulties with grace and charm. He worked over his translations with great care, but his comments in English on Buddhism and Zen came from his own illuminated mind and heart without premeditation. For Sokei-an, real individuality, the authenticity of one's spontaneous response, are what counted. This was found right under one's nose in the world of human relations, in the mind-to-mind transactions between people. The experience of seeing one's original nature and of direct communication was at the heart of Sokei-an's Zen. Sokei-an demonstrated this principle, not through any system or controlled circumstances, but by manifesting his own present mind and by bringing others into it. Sokei-an felt the shortcoming of contemporary Zen was that students did not think that their everyday life was Zen itself. Every moment tests you in action. If you do not grasp this pivotal point of Zen, you may never find your true existence. You may think Zen is a theory that makes you wise, but it is a religion that makes you very plain and pure. The final words of Sokei-an were, "You must consider very intensely what you are doing every moment, not depending on any other way. It is the only way."

Here before you are many of the rough jewels scattered as Sokei-an spoke intimately about his own life. Sokei-an once said that Zen is a "long-lived being." Like so many before him he had broken into Zen and stayed in it. When he was a young boy with a fishing pole, he stopped at an old temple. There was a Zen monk giving a lecture to the stones in the garden. Sokei-an listened, although he couldn't understand. At twenty-three, after Sokei-an had become a Zen student, he happened to pass by the same temple. There were two hundred well-dressed people from Tokyo listening to this same monk. Sokei-an's teacher said to him: "Say anything you want. Don't mind the audience. Stones hear—a stone may hear!" Sokei-an spoke to the rock of Manhattan, and now he would certainly smile to see an autobiography entitled *Holding the Lotus to the Rock*. He would be surprised to find that so many of his spoken teachings and funny stories about his life remain. He gave them entirely to the moment.

Michael Hotz
The First Zen Institute of America
New York City, Spring 2002

# I Was a Dreamer When I Was a Child

When I was a child, I asked my father where I came from. My mother had told me she had picked me up from somewhere and carried me into the house. I worried, so I asked my father. "I found you in that tree branch." Everyone has this question. It is a gate, an entrance to Zen.

I was passed from lap to lap by my aunts. At first I did not recognize the faces of my aunts. It was always my mother. Later, I made distinctions among them. A man recognizes the distinctions without being conscious of recognizing them. This function is naturally given to us. It is very mysterious. In this darkness without beginning, the unconscious creative activity begins. This creative activity itself becomes aware of its own activity. It is called consciousness.

My first memory was of crying, and in this crying voice I woke to this world. I was perhaps two years of age. I slowly realized why I was crying. I was crying because my mother was in the kitchen. She was not beside me, therefore I cry. I found myself in this crying attitude long after I was grown.

> Cool shadow of the willow tree
> Sweeps the weathered garden porch
> Whose baby are you?
> That your mother might have fear
> Of your deep slumber!

Sleeping mind is different from awakened mind. It is as though you are sleeping in the broad daylight under the sun. You look at the sun with your eyes, but you are snoring. That is life. Your wisdom gate must awaken so that you can see both sides at once. Men and women, born from darkness without beginning come forth and look at the outside. From empirical intuition, it takes a long time to find that time and space are the body of consciousness. I saw the outside when my mother gave me birth, but it was not until I met a Zen master that the "skin of my eye" was peeled off, and I could see this state of reality. Now I am in it and I cannot get out. I take life and death, and I "play" in this state of manifested reality.

My father always put me to bed. From the time I was three years old, he told me bedtime stories in Chinese. So the sound of the Chinese words was familiar to me from my earliest memories. At five, he began to teach me Chinese, and writing those characters was my work as a child. When I was crying and nagging my mother, my father would say, "Keep your mind in shape!"

I was a dreamer. I liked to read fairy tales, and when I was alone I was always dreaming. Everyone living in this world who speaks of the transcendental world thinks the transcendental world must be like a fairy world in these stories, and they wish to find it and be absorbed in that ecstasy.

A child of four or five years is really in the empty state, but the child does not keep the present emptiness in his mind. A child's mind is free. A child's mind is divine, not nailed down or nailed up on the wall—not crucified. It is free, living, and walking on the earth, not killed between two ideas of bad and good, of time and space, not crushed between two robbers and two bandits. When I came to America, I realized that people here don't do that, don't care what thoughts run about in their brains. Their minds are really in a primitive state. If you have such a mind, look into it and find what it is.

I think about the old days, about how my father educated me. After supper he would call me to his chair and educate me. He taught me what it is to be a human being. In the West, mothers used to teach children. These days fathers and mothers put the baby to bed and go out dancing somewhere. The child goes to school, and the schoolteacher gets a salary for dumping out knowledge. No one teaches the child how to develop the qualities of a human being.

My father was a Shinto priest and served the sea god. His shrine was in Southern Japan by the seaside. Warm currents always washed the piles of the shrine gate. I was born in the small city of the shrine, named Konpira. Many pilgrims came to my shrine, where there was the big horse race of the spring festival, under the cherry blossoms. There was the big boat race of the autumn festival, after the typhoon season. I heard many splendid explanations of Shintoism from the priests. I remember many ceremonies and many principles of Shintoism.

When I was a small boy, I asked my father, "What is in the

deepest part of the shrine?" My father said "God." There are many legends about the sacred mirrors of Shintoism. When the sun goddess sent her descendants down to the Central Land of the Reedy Sea (Japan), from the plane of high heaven, she passed to him three treasures—a sword, a mirror, and a jewel. She said about the sword: "When you see this sword, think of my body." She said about the mirror: "When you see this mirror, think of my soul, and when you see this jewel, think of my love." The sword's meaning is wisdom, the mirror's meaning is consciousness, and the jewel's meaning is movement.

As a child, I had faith in the Shinto God. The Shinto God has no physical body. It is omnipresent, omnipotent, and omniscient. It is not localized in any particular place. To my childish mind, *Kami*, the spirit which animates all things, was wonderful and infinite. According to the Shinto faith, the Shinto God protects us in every way. A Shintoist has no idea of a God who punishes; he believes only that if he commits any errors God will feel sorry about it. Neither my father nor I even thought of Kami in human form or as having the nature of human beings. It came to my mind when I was five years old that God is universal vast space, infinite time and infinite power.

One day, after a festival was going on and every priest was busy in the shrine, I had a chance to slip out from the big room given over to ceremonies into the deepest part to see God. I thought of myself just as a mouse, because the hall was so dark and so long and so still. I saw candlelight at the end of the hall, its long flames palpitating toward the high ceiling. There was a screen hanging down, dividing the human world from God. My heart was palpitating just like the candle's fire. It was too sublime for a mouse. Many times I hesitated to roll up the screen and get in. I bowed many times, like the priest, and recited a spell I had always heard from my father. Then I crept in. There, inside the deepest part of the shrine, it was very dark. I could not see anything, although a faint light behind the screen shone at my back. I searched out the square box on the square pedestal, and I found a round white thing lying on the box. I gazed into it. My eye made out some form, the form of a face that was startled. Really, there was just a round mirror in the darkness, like the spirit, which the Japanese say is round and lying in our deepest bosom. After growing up, I confessed this adventure to my father. "Yes," he said, "I know there is the mirror, but I have not been there yet."

From 1890 to 1894, my father was attached to a school of Shinto priests in Sendai. He was a specialist in the ancient Japanese language and taught me from my earliest childhood. There was a university there. In Sendai, the samurai spirit was still flourishing. My father was an instructor for Shinto priests. That knowledge was not in books, not handed down as belonging to Shinto.

In the evening when I did not come home early, my father always told me, "Beware, my child! The unseen evil spirits in the air will kidnap you!" And then, sitting on the verandah in the evening, seeing dust in the air, I asked my father why I couldn't see the spirits there. "Spirits," he told me, "are thinner than air: like gas, you cannot see them. But they are in the air, and they will snatch you away from your own existence." "I wonder, father," I said, "can the evil spirits which have such etheric bodies snatch our physical bodies?" "No, child, they cannot snatch the physical body, but the mental body they can take away when children are fighting, so come home very early!" Today we think, "Oh, those old notions are just superstitions." But from our own angle, it is an ancient expression of something. We can express the same things in an entirely different way today.

When I was a child, I would go to a Buddhist temple in Sendai, where my father lived and taught in the University. In the summer, there were ten nights in July when the monks gave a series of ten lectures on anything. After the harvest, the farmers have nothing to do, and they accept Buddhism for only ten nights. The monks, among other things, told ghosts stories, and we children were afraid to go home!

A young Shinto boy came to a priest and asked a question: "Is water a sentient being?" The priest said "No." "Is fire a sentient being?" "No." The child said, "I cannot understand. You always said the sun was a sentient being—goddess mother of the world. Why is not fire or water a sentient being?" The priest said, "Show me water. Show me fire." The child showed water in a cup. "Is it living? " "No, but it is not a dead thing. It is living in some way," the priest said. A famous answer in Shinto says: "When you pick up things from the earth and ask me this, then the things are dead. When you return them to the earth, they are living."

When I was young, I said to my teacher: "I think the most beautiful moment of my life is when I am sleeping." "Yes, it is," he said. "And then when I get home," I said, "I talk to my mother, and it seems that this is the true time." From day to evening is the true time; there is no false time. That Zen koan— "Depending upon nothing"—it is a trick to cut through to quick realization. And then every moment is a true moment.

I watched my dreams very carefully, day and night, and I dug deep into my mind. My mind was chaotic—it didn't obey my control. I attempted to make daily notes of my dreams. I kept a notebook and pencil near my pillow and tried to write them down. Then I would go off to sleep again. My mother always said: "What are you doing? Stop that nonsense and go to sleep. Don't be bothered by your dreams." It usually happened that when I had carefully arranged my notebook and pencil and gone to bed, either I didn't dream anything or I didn't awake. If I had made no arrangements, I would be sure to dream, but by the time I had awakened, jumped from my bed, searched around for the notebook and pencil, and finally found them, I had forgotten what I had dreamed—I had lost my dream.

This training was the beginning of my meditation. Finally I trained myself to memorize my dreams so exactly that I could note all the details down in my book. I would have had to write ten or fifteen pages every day. My poet friend laughed at me: "Most of it is your imagination, your own creation. You have lost the boundary between your dreams and your imagination. Stop this nonsense!" I realized that it was so. But I still use that training.

When I was young, Christ came to Japan. Certainly those missionaries took our neck and whipped our rear to throw us into Christianity! Certainly we went to their school, for at Christmas they gave us souvenirs. Perhaps they were not great teachers—perhaps not teachers at all in their own country! I went to a Christian church that appeared on my street, Waseda Street. All the children of Waseda Street went there and helped. Finally the children had some quarrel with the pastor's wife and left the church. For three months the church had no adherents.

There was a child who was the son of a Confucian. His father was teaching Confucianism to a prince. This child went home and told his father that he was a sinner. The father, feeling that his family had been disparaged (in which case he must either commit *hara-kiri* or resign from his teacher's position), went to the pastor. We children laughed and finally asked, "We come from good families; our conduct is good, our fathers are gentlemen and our mothers are ladies—how can we be sinners?" The answer: "Those who do not know God are sinners. Confess your ignorance to God, and He will forgive your sins." We carried the pastor's answer to the temple in our street. The *Osho*, or teacher, was there and said, "The Christian view is right. Ignorance is a sin." I came back home and asked my father, a Shinto priest, about this. My father just laughed—"It is false. Everyone on earth is pure!"

Pantheism is not bad. It gives us a reason to understand the world. It does not contradict science, arithmetic, optics, dynamics. Pantheism is a true religion. I still believe it is true. We had to think about that teaching, which was given to us by the Western Christian missionaries. We were scared, and then we slowly came to our senses and came out of it. I was born the son of a Shinto priest and did not believe in it from the first day. I knew that human prayer through a human throat cannot be heard by God; that the prayer that can be heard is daily life. I knew it when I was five years old, a true-thinking child.

When I was a small boy, I sometimes went to a Buddhist temple, and there I saw a screen on which a picture of hell was painted. It was a dreadful sight to a child—swords, broadswords, wolves, bloodhounds, and fire. In those dreadful hells, the lost souls suffer in endless torment, while the demons of hell who are torturing the dead spirits look quite comfortable, smiling with great amusement as they torture the dead spirit of a human being.

*Sokatsu Shaku, teacher of Sokei-an Sasaki.*

I was the son of a Shinto priest and Shinto has no hell, so I did not believe that such a place exists under the earth. I thought that this was a product of man's imagination. I mischievously thought of a question to ask the monk. When I met him on the verandah, I asked him, "Why do those demons of hell not suffer while all those human souls are suffering?" The monk, knowing that I was the son of a Shinto priest, answered, "Son, you ask a good question, but you must know that these dead spirits still have no conscience and so do not suffer." I came

*Imakita Kosen, teacher of Soyen Shaku.*

*Soyen Shaku*

home and asked my father. He said, "Both good and bad men have conscience." I was much amused by my father's answer.

After I attained the wisdom of Buddhism, I asked the same question of an old monk. He said: "There is an answer to that question in a *shastra* written by Asanga, who said, 'Those demons of hell see no hell. Hell can be seen by those who have committed a sin. Hell exists subjectively. Those demons and the King of Hell may live in hell, but for them it is not a place of torment, because they did not commit any crime or sin. Their tormenting of the dead spirits of the sinful men is a sign of their compassion for those sinful people.'"

I was a little puzzled. I could not understand at first, but I think that all officers in jail believe that they are very kind to prisoners. They are living in jail, but they do not suffer. Judges who convict criminals are not suffering, but the criminal is. I searched out that passage in Asanga and found that he explained that Hell exists in a man's mind only; it does not exist anywhere objectively. The struggle in men's minds is hell. When I was a boy, I asked a Buddhist monk if he realized that underground there isn't such a place as hell. The monk said, "Ah, but look into your own mind! Something there tortures you."

I met a Zen monk. I looked at him and smiled and looked at him again. I tried to search his mind. I felt, "He is not thinking anything at all!" I smiled again. He did not smile back to me. It was my first contact with a Zen master. Later I went to Ryomo temple and met Zen master Sokatsu Shaku. He looked at me with his great eyes and that was all.

# When My Father Died

*I*n my father's day, the western feudal lords revolted against the Tokugawa regime. They changed the feudal system and installed a new government. They took away the two swords from the samurai and made the samurai commoners. Swordsmiths lost their jobs entirely. No one bought new swords any more, and old swords were melted to make chains to fasten dogs which came from Western countries and were very precious at that time. Swordsmiths had to change their occupations to make shovels and pickaxes for the farmers. They were terribly ashamed and refused to take such inferior positions. They committed *hara-kiri* and died. They had to exist as dead men, but they avoided coming down to beat shovels.

I was born in the fifteenth year of Meiji's government. In the eighth year of Meiji, the order was given to Buddhist monks: Hereafter you don't need to observe commandments. Eat meat,

35

marry, do anything you want. Buddhism still existed up to my twelfth or thirteenth year in Japan, but then overwhelming waves of Western culture rolled into Japan, and there were terrible economic struggles. No pure love anymore when economic life comes into human life. Today we have to exist economically as the slave of money. This is wrong; it must be wiped out. We must go back to the Buddha's way, the middle way.

When I was a child, there was much food in the mountains, in the sea. I didn't come back home for my lunch. I dug clams and oysters and ate them. The Eastern idea is to live without working. The tree gives food, the mountain gives food, the sea gives food. So long as we are supported, we don't need civilization. But when a country is industrialized, there is no more natural food.

When I was a child, I was crazy about catching shrimp—and crazy about eating them too. Every day I was down by the water catching shrimp and bringing them home for my mother to cook for me. One day when no one was at home, I came in with some shrimp, and I discovered that through observing my mother carefully I knew already, without knowing I knew, how to cook shrimp. So I put some water in one of my mother's pots and boiled it, and I cooked those shrimp. They were delicious. But when my mother came home—"What! You have cooked shrimp in my best pot, and I have to take the shrimp smell out! There is my shrimp pot—nothing else is ever cooked in it."

I was like any child who, when it does something big, likes to do it again. He thinks any pot is a shrimp pot when he wants to cook shrimp. So several times when nobody was home I took any pot and cooked my shrimp in it. One day my mother came home with a new pot in her hand. "Here, Yeita," she said, "is a shrimp-cooking pot for you. Cook your shrimp in it and wash the pot and put it away. It is yours; nobody else will touch it." I was very delighted with that small cooking pot that was mine. I always used it, and I washed it too and put it away. I think by that pot I first realized "personal property" when I was a child.

When I was a boy, I was looking for drinking water in the temple near where I was fishing. I left my rod outside and went inside. There was only one monk in this little old temple and one old woman. He was giving a lecture to one old woman and stones! I understood he was giving a lecture, and I stayed till it was over. I did not understand a word! At twenty, I entered the monastery. Then, when I was twenty-three years old and studying Zen, I was passing through some place, and I saw many dressed-up ladies and gentlemen going into a temple. It was the same temple, the same monk, and an audience of two hundred! I was impressed. Ten years before, he was giving a lecture to stones. Now the bus brought people from Tokyo, transplanting life on those rocks. Later my teacher said, "Say anything you want. Don't mind the audience. Stones hear—a stone may hear! If there are four hundred, speak as only to one."

When I was about twelve, my father went to the village shrine of Goi, on a small river near Murata in Shimosa in Chiba Prefecture. My father was just fishing around; he was not teaching. I saw a beautiful fishing apparatus and asked my mother to purchase it. She shook her head and said, "No." I went to my father. He said "I made a beautiful rod for you. Why do you wish to buy the one in the store window?" I went to my uncle and invented a lie and borrowed the money and bought the rod from the shop. Later I read a pamphlet about how to swim. Then I went to practice and sank down very quickly!

When I was twelve, my father sent me to an English group school. I started with ABC. When I came to live in San Francisco, I had studied English for about fifteen years. We used the *National English Readers*, old Civil War readers. By the time I came to America I was on number four *National English Reader*! On examination day, before I went to school in the morning, I would close my books and go to my seat to meditate. If, in the examination, a very difficult problem appeared on the blackboard and I was in a quandary, I meditated to quench the palpitation of my heart, for I had found that my brain worked better after meditation.

Once my father was sick and sent me down to close up the shrine and put out the candles. It was difficult for me to blow those high things out, so I took them down and put the candle-flame into water. Next morning he tried to light the candles. They were wet and would not light. He was so angry he would not speak to me for two weeks. I was sent away from home to my uncle. My father lost his temper at particular times and over particular things when anyone stepped on his robe or cut the weeds with his samurai sword. I knew those things bothered him, and I did them anyway. I insulted his position, and it was sacred to him. Why did he blame me? He lost his temper before God, and I was the cause. I was sent to my uncle for two weeks.

My uncle hit me, but I had a good vacation. I was thirteen years old then. My uncle listened to how I came to him. Then he hit me here, in my jaw. I had to think seriously. For one whole day I was in a bad humor. My aunt realized it was under my skin. "How can you, Yeita?" she said. "You are a shame to the whole family of Shinto." I was a modern child with no reverence.

When I was about thirteen or fourteen, I was walking a country road alone. I met a boy. He looked at me. He looked about like me. It was a wonderful experience. I felt I was not alone.

When I was fifteen years old, my father was very ill. Another Shinto priest told me to go to the shrine and bring back holy water to sprinkle on my father's face. The moment I opened the shrine, I felt a great wall between God and myself. Should I offer prayer for my father's life? I realized that I was not with Kami. I tried to tear down the wall, to enter the bosom of God, but it was in vain. I could not penetrate to that God. He wasn't in the shrine, and he wasn't in heaven. I could not pray to him. So I came back empty handed. The priest said to me, "Why didn't you bring back the holy water?" I said, "No use." To that day I had believed the water was sacred—but not that day! It was old stale water with dust in it. When I really needed a God, I found a gap between me and him. It gave me a question! Fifteen years old! I was restless. Born in a Shinto priest's house, from infancy I had no doubt that I was in the bosom of God. But when I really needed a God, I could not reach him: he wasn't in the shrine, he wasn't in heaven. I couldn't save my father by supplication.

In 1897 father died. Two days later, the official appointment came to the great shrine at Ise. It was read to the dead body. The village people begged me to go to the Shinto University and take my fathers' place. I walked out among the big trees behind the shrine at Goi. Then, the pale winter sky among the trees!

After father's burial, there was in my mind a question: "How has my father's soul been settled?" The great sky among the trees understood, but it was connected with my first koan and when I saw a dead horse in New York.

My father's body was buried very near the town. I came back

from the funeral and passed through the temple yard covered by pine trees. Childishly, I wondered—"Where is my father now?" I could not believe that his soul was existing anywhere on the earth or under it. I looked at the sky and thought, "My father's soul is scattered all over, like heat or light." And then, as I stumbled over the root of a pine tree—"If my father is everywhere, he will be in this pine tree root, on the tip of my tongue and the tip of my toe!"

I was a child of a Shinto priest, and from seven years old I saw it was foolish to supplicate, "Oh, God in heaven, I wish to have five dollars in the morning to buy a new hat!" Indirect religion is something for sleeping minds. I returned home without tears. Today I realize that fifteen-year-old boy was not quite a fool! He had gathered all his philosophy at the grammar school and come to that conclusion. Quite reasonable, wasn't it? In my Buddhism today, I should say that it has not developed much beyond that fifteen-year-old boy. Of course, being a child of a Shinto priest, I had heard about the "soul" every day. It was, to me, a big question.

# I Think There Is Someone Living in My Attic

When I first looked into my mind, I realized that my mind was flowing always. It was like peeking into a dirty pond. I realized something was moving inside, but I couldn't see the bottom. I am sure that many people, mature people forty to fifty years old, have never examined their minds, have never known what is going on in their minds. I made an attempt to keep a record of my mind activity from morning to evening, seeking to find out what I was thinking. I wrote ten pages a day. After a time, I gave it up. There was too much. I destroyed it. Of course my mother found it and laughed at me. At the age of twenty, when I came to Zen, I realized the value of introspection.

Of course I was annoyed with my mother after my father's death—crying in the night. I so despised her! Why did she have to surrender to that agony? After I came into the temple, I practiced introspection. I understood my mother's morbid dreaming,

*Photo sent to Mary Farkas from*
*Elizabeth Sharp of Sokei-an during his*
*Greenwich Village days.*

and not only that—I realized also that the morbid, flowing mind must be external. It is like a man sitting in his chair and tapping on the table . . . insane! But you have controlling power, you have conscious memory, and you can live sanely.

I was eighteen years old when I realized that I was thinking something all the time. I said to my mother, "I think someone is living in my attic!" "Therefore you are insane," she said.

I lost my cousin when I was very young. She was a nice young girl, and I stayed with her until the very end—I was always with her. When she was very sick I would say, "No, you are not dying." And she would cling to me and say, "Oh, oh, I am falling down, constantly down, down." Fear! I have seen many people dying suddenly, scratching the floor, scratching anywhere, in fear. Shameful death! Thanks to Buddhism, this need not come if awakening has come first.

After my father's death, all his clothes were mine. We were quite poor and to save buying me clothes, my mother said, "Wear your father's robes, child." So, in some park or on some beach, wearing those samurai robes too long for me, some old servant, some feudal servant of another family, recognizing the Sasaki symbol, would in passing salute the robe with its insignia. He would not know me. He would salute the robe, not me!

I went with my mother to Yokohama where I worked in a woodcarving factory. Before settling there, I went on a walking trip through the Japanese Alps. I made my way by temple carving in the villages, earning about thirty-five cents a day. I walked for one year through the Japanese Alps, from village to village, my tools on my back, going from one temple to the next. In China or Japan, monasteries are built on mountaintops or on the edges of cliffs. You can see a thousand miles before your eyes. In winter, when the valley is covered with snow, you feel you are in a world of silver. No color is before your eyes. In the valley it is so quiet. In the daytime when the monks are meditating, if there is any sound in the temple, it will be only that of a mouse or a rat.

I had my carving tools, and I earned my way by temple carving through the Japanese Alps. But I had to sharpen my tools. It took me four or five years to learn. And to sharpen my tools I must have a stone—a very fine stone, very expensive. I was without any money to buy it. "Go to see your uncle," my mother told me, "he has plenty of money. Take him some of your carvings—ask him to look at them, and tell him what you need. Wear your father's robe and pay a call on him." So I put on my father's robe, not his priest's robe, of course. My father was a very big man, and I but a boy of sixteen or seventeen. I was too short for his robe, and it trailed behind me as I bowed before my uncle.

He looked at my work and asked me many questions. He looked at my tools, and asked me if I intended to make wood-carving my life work. "I wish to," I said, "but I have a hindrance. My tools are not well sharpened. I haven't got a good stone." "What kind of sharpening stone do you wish for?" he asked me. "I wish for the finest," I told him, "the sharpening stone that comes only from your native province." I do not know if it is really so, but perhaps his love for his native province was flattered a little.

He turned my wooden image, looking at it very carefully from every angle. Then he said, "Very well, child, go back home and be a good son to your mother. I will order a sharpening stone from my province, one of the very finest. Go back home and wait till the postman brings it to you. It will be sent to you personally." I waited for many days—two, three weeks. Then one day it came, addressed to me, "Mr. Yeita Sasaki." It was a sharpening stone of the very finest quality. I began at once to sharpen my tools. I was very happy that day.

In my own view, in my youth I was using my brain, and later my mind and heart, and now I am trying to use my own nature. Where you place the center of your activity makes your attitude to your own life different. You must understand this. When Japanese boys study, they have to draw Japanese characters with a brush. Children use their fingertips to write, and then when they study character writing, the teacher says, "Don't touch your hand to the table. Hold your hand this way." And the child says, "How can I draw this way?" And the teacher says, "Put your strength in your shoulder and let your hand relax. Don't move your hand or elbow, but draw from the shoulder, and when it is a big character, draw from the hip." When I was studying oil painting, my teacher said, "Don't hold the brush so tightly; hold it very lightly." In such a way hold your mind and heart, very lightly, and keep your strength in your nature. Do you know how to do this? I am sure you do not!

I am not an expert in golf, but I observe there is this movement from the hip. If one drives from the shoulder, the ball does not drive right. And in boxing, I observe that boxers give the blows from the body. All art has this knack. When I was studying wood carving, I was afraid I would hit my hand instead of the wood, for I struck from my elbow. My teacher said, "Use your own brain!" If you use your own brain, you will make many mistakes. Use it all—mind, brain, and heart—but use it relaxed. Tension kills function. It fills the brain, and you become like a squeezed lemon.

One day, by chance I came upon the book *Shinbikyô* by Mori Ogai. The word *shinbi* (appreciation of the beautiful) attracted my attention and encouraged me to read the book, but I was not sufficiently educated so could not make anything of it. I was so disappointed at not being able to understand it that I read it over and over again, until the book became worn and dirty. Finally, I began to understand it. What pleased me most about the book was that it made me realize that my job as a sculptor was important. If my job was important, I felt that I had to study sculpture properly.

In 1901, I entered Takamura Koun's studio. He took me on as a house student in his home. I stayed there off and on. I was

*Takamaru Koun, Sokei-an's sculpture teacher, and his students, circa 1900. Sokei-an is leaning against a tree staring off to the left.*

accepted by Takamura as one of eighteen students. I entered the Imperial Academy of Art in Tokyo, but worked in Takamura's studio.

Once in my art school, we had a female model who had a baby, and every now and then she had to leave us and go feed it. But while she was a model for us, her breasts dripped milk, and one of us held a cup under her breast and caught the milk and the students tasted it—it was very sweet. But it went a little further! Some students sucked the milk from her! And then the teacher came in! Oh, he was furious! "What is this that is going on! Gentlemen! What are you doing! This is terrible! I shall lose my position! Do you want that? Then never do such a thing again!" Noon came and we were told that the principal of the school wished to see us. Such commotion! "Are you children? What have you done! Where is your morality? How old are you?" We were twenty-three, twenty-one, some older. "Must we educate you again in morality?" "Well," we said, "we could not see it as immoral. We just wished to taste that milk. We had forgotten what it tasted like!" But he said it was immoral for him, for the school, for us. From his point of view it was immoral, but to us there was no immorality. However, we said we would observe the rule and not do it again!

When I was young and studying wood carving, I always realized that someone was living in my attic, carving something independently. Someone was independently thinking while I carved. Whenever I did anything—walking on the street, going to bed, working—this fellow in the attic was thinking his own thoughts! Sometimes I put my tools away and cooperated in his thinking. I became acquainted, then intimate with him. I thought he was an old man and called him a philosopher, a queer philosopher three thousand years old. Gradually he occupied my whole house and drove out the woodcarver. Then one day the philosopher disappeared and I discovered my self. When the philosopher snatched away all the property of the woodcarver, he disappeared and I was born! I still visit the philosopher occasionally.

When I was seventeen years old, I was associating with other students, talking about philosophy. Some German philosophy had come into my country and was translated. The students read it and every night in this boarding house they gathered to argue and discuss and dispute, and in the end to fight, even give one another black eyes! They worked hard, strove very hard to find the truth, but they thought the truth existed only in words.

At seventeen or eighteen, we open a doubtful eye: Why do we live? Where do we come from? Were we here before? Where do we go? If we have no such period of seeking, I should say that we are sleeping. This questioning comes to every young man's eye before he even opens it to sex. Sex, like a flower, will come later, but first a leaf appears. It is the questioning of everything. This is wisdom curing ignorance.

My mother thought I had gone crazy. I wrote the character "tree" on paper, then destroyed it and brought in a real tree, hung it on the wall. My mother said, "What has happened to this poor child?" I fell into sickness that lasted until I went into the monastery.

One student suggested, "Why don't you look into Zen?" In Tokyo, I worked at the parcel post office till 1:00 AM, then talked from 1:00 to 5:00 AM. A law student there gave me four words—subjective, objective, abstract, concrete. I began to think till I was crazy. What were those words? This made me what I am today.

To find one's self is very interesting work. Someone is in me. Who is this one? To locate him in one's self, to detect him, to find his nature is wonderful work. I was puzzled by the division of subjectivity and objectivity. I ran outside and closed the door, thinking I was in objectivity. Then I ran into the house and closed the door—closed my eyes—and thought I was in subjectivity. Westerners think that what is before the eyes is objective and what is behind the eyes, subjective. But Buddhists think everything on the shelf of consciousness is objective.

I did not learn the practice of Samadhi in a monastery, but from my art teacher. When I was learning to paint the sea, our teacher asked his students not to sketch the waves on the seashore or to copy the waves in the ancient masterpieces. "Without brush or palette," he said, "go alone to the seashore and sit down on the sands. Then practice this: forget yourself until even your own existence is forgotten and you are entirely absorbed in the motion of the waves."

*Woodcarving (title unknown) by Sokei-an.*

So day after day in the summertime, we would go to the seashore, to the so-called "Ninety-Nine Mile Beach" near Tokyo on the Pacific Ocean. We would stay at the beach all day long. When we came back in the evening to our lodging-houses and hotels in the city, we felt as though we were still at the seashore listening to the pounding surf. Some young artists would stay there a week, then returning to their studios would seize their brushes and paint waves in the very rhythm of the sea. This is our way of art. This is also what we call Samadhi—you transform yourself into the object you are confronting. There is a famous Japanese artist, Sosen, who painted nothing but monkeys. He was living with monkeys in his house, he was living like a monkey, and finally he understood the thought of monkeys. At last, when he took his brush in his hand to paint monkeys, all the monkeys came and stood behind him and criticized him. So there are many kinds and degrees of Samadhi.

Zen is an art form. I found this knack of going back to the bosom of nature because I was an artist and worshipped Nature. From this feeling, I entered Zen very quickly. When I was about nineteen, I studied sculpture of the Egyptians, Greeks, Romans, and Renaissance; then modern French work, and finally returned to Oriental art. I came to modern art from life. I was then sketching outside, carrying my canvas under my arm. How I adored nature! I surrendered absolutely. The farmers thought I was crazy, seeing me join my hands and kneel down to a little brook, a tree or a small flower. I came into religion through art. I knew there must be another way, through daily life, but from that humility before great nature I came to the gate of religion, of Buddhism.

One day I was looking at a lotus pond in the autumn. All the petals were brown and the leaves and stems were dying. And yet the whole thing was really very beautiful. I could not put in or take out one single stem. I bowed down to Nature and tried to understand. If I could solve this mystery, I would know something. This question haunted my mind for a long time. I solved the question after I went into the Zen monastery.

One day I went out to sketch with my easel and palette. I made the colors, looked and tried to sketch, but I simply could not work. That was when I gave up art and went into the monastery. There I found the answer to the question which opened the gate. When I understood, art no longer lured me. I knew that art did not matter.

# This Very Mind Is the Seat of Zen Practice

*I* had the sickness of doubt in my youth. I could not read, study, or eat. I was shivering and pale—they called me "grasshopper-legs" and "blue-spike." Somehow I had to settle the question! I was a spoiled child, thought no one was like myself. I was that type of young man. It was not until after I was thirty-seven that I came into a world of some sunshine, where I could enjoy the outside and associate with friends. Before that, I was ill-natured and quick-tempered. I really felt that the earth filled up the mind and was the end of joy. Sometimes I wondered how anyone could live and what would happen after death. Reincarnation was just talk; transmigration was just talk; karma was just talk. I had five senses, but how were they connected after death? What senses would stay and what would go? So many questions! What was love? What was morality?

It was like peeling the skin of an orange. I did very careful, very tedious work. Otherwise, I thought, there was no use living. "I am doing something very important, but will I starve to death?" Even so, I had to get everything settled and come to terms with myself. Without this, I could not go on. It was like settling one's account at the end of the month. If you cannot find the error, you cannot sleep. The question of everyday life is the same: you must think deeply about it, for no one else's sake but for your own; otherwise, your life is just nonsense. If I don't know what will happen after death, how can I lie down comfortably to die?

If you practice this Zen meditation for many years, what will happen to you then? When I was young, I was afraid my landlady would put me out because my mother did not send me any money. So I meditated in my room. My landlady saw me and smiled! The money came and I paid my landlady, and I asked her why she smiled.

"Child, I saw you meditating. I knew you had no money!" Sometimes my mother did not send me money—no money for three days! I had some coppers, and I bought a loaf of bread and some sugar. The daughter of the grocery man said to me, "Are you hungry?" "No, give me my bread and sugar!" And I ate it and I slept mindlessly for three days! We cannot be mindless when we are living in the topmost branch of our tree of soul. But when we come back to the root of this tree, we can be a mindless man.

When I conceived the question, "What is life after all? What is life for? Why I am I studying art?" the value of everything disappeared. "I cannot work. It is meaningless! I cannot live so. Today, tomorrow—I cannot study art without meaning. There must be meaning. Must be something! I go to school and I bow to the teacher—what for? I bow to my mother—what for?" To build a house upon the ground, you must lay a foundation; without a foundation, what can you build? You must build your life upon some foundation.

My doubt came when I was nineteen years old. I thought that everyone must be the same, that everyone must pass through this agony. But now I know that this is not true at all. Others do not care about such things. They do not care if life has meaning or no meaning. They work because they must have money to eat, must eat to live, must live to work, must work to make money, must make money to eat! I cannot look at life in such a way. I cannot live in such a way. Therefore I live fighting against agony. To an honest man, this is the fundamental agony. He doesn't care whether he has money, whether he is poor or rich, famous or obscure. If he has no true foundation of life, his life doesn't mean anything at all!

Talk doesn't mean a thing. Soul or mind, whatever you call it, is just a name. In the Zen school, talking is no good. A name is like the menu of a restaurant. If you don't eat the food itself, how can you be nourished? If you are sick and get a prescription from a doctor and you don't take it, how can you get well? When you talk about soul, mind, or consciousness you must prove what it is!

I became a Buddhist. My knowledge was growing and I, a skeptic, had to conquer my doubt. I suffered and entered into Buddhism in order to conquer this doubt. I had been sent to a Zen master, my teacher Sokatsu at Ryomo-an. I said two or three words. He said, "There is no truth in the word! The word speaks about something. You open your mouth and the word has gone away. There is something that was spoken by the word. What was that something?" I gasped and went away. If I cannot speak, truth has gone away. There is no truth left in my mind. The only truth that is left to me is this body and this mind.

During the Meiji era, the true practice of Buddhism had atrophied. Imakita Kosen determined that the way to rescue it was by recruiting talented people from society at large. Kosen seems to have taken as keen an interest in the promulgation of Zen among laymen as in the lay-education of Zen Buddhist monks. During the many years he remained at Engakuji, that temple became the center of the lay study of Zen. Many students from the newly founded universities of Tokyo, which was not far, flocked to its dynamic master. Kosen was a man of great stature and of prodigious strength. Soon after his arrival in Kamakura, Kosen began to hold meditation meetings in Tokyo in the spring and autumn at the request of a group of distinguished gentlemen, among whom were Tesshu Yamaoka, a famous fencing master and a member of the Emperor's bodyguard, and Chomin Nakae, one of the first students of the Western science of physics. Kosen called his group *Ryomokyo-kai*. *Ryomokyo* means the abandonment of the concepts both of subjectivity and of objectivity. *Kai* means society or association. The formation of this group was of great importance to my own life, as will soon be seen. Among those who came to study under Kosen during the later years of his life was a young layman called Sekibutsu Koji. Sekibutsu means "Stone Buddha," and Koji means "lay-disciple." Kosen passed away, but Sekibutsu continued his Zen study under Soyen Shaku, Kosen's heir.

Soyen Shaku was a unique figure among the Buddhist priests of his day. Certainly he was not one of those who merely followed the traditional attitudes. He was a graduate of Keio

Gijiku, now Keio University, which had been established by Yukichi Fukuzawa on his return from America in 1866 as a school for the study of western culture and learning. Soyen had been sent to Keio Gijiku by his teacher Kosen, who seems early to have recognized the genius of his disciple and to have foreseen the influence he was destined to wield in the world of modern Zen. So during the early years of Meiji, while other Buddhists were sleeping comfortably pillowed on the customs of the feudal period, Soyen was studying Western thought and culture. Kosen was also an unusual man in that he chose for his disciple an education which was both modern and ancient.

Soyen first studied Zen under Ekkei Zenji, then came to Kosen. He was indeed a genius! At an early age, the secret principles of Zen were transmitted to him. I have heard from my teacher this story about him. One day Kosen said to a lay-student who had just passed a certain koan after three years of struggle, "You have spent three years on this koan. Yesterday I gave this koan to Soyen. This morning he passed it! He is a born Bodhisattva." In the Zen school it is very seldom that a teacher extols a student.

Soyen Shaku became abbot of Engaku Temple and was one of the great men of Zen Buddhism in the Meiji period. He was the possessor of fiery eyes and iron guts. My first interview with him took place when I was in my twenties. My friend introduced me to the abbot. The first moment of this interview the abbot's two shining eyes pierced my mind through and through. I stood in silence, aghast! The abbot questioned me about what I wished to become. I replied, "I am studying art." "What are you studying?" "I am learning how to carve Buddhistic statues." "Who is your teacher?" "Koun Takamura." He looked into my eyes again and said, "Carve a Buddha statue for me when you become a famous artist." And he gave us tea and cakes. Never in my life have I met another man who possessed such shining eyes.

When Sekibutsu shaved his head, Soyen gave him the name Sokatsu, which means "energetic," and still later when Soyen adopted him as son, he gave him his "family" name of Shaku. It was this Sokatusu Shaku who was my Zen master. Sokatsu Shaku was barely twenty-nine when he finished his Zen. After his return from Siam and Burma, Soyen summoned him one day and told him that the time had come for him to promulgate Zen.

"You have acquired the great wisdom of Buddhism. Now you must complete the Four Great Vows which you made and turn the wheel of supplication for the benefit of others," he said. "The assemblage which Kosen Osho called Ryomokyo-kai has dispersed, Sokatsu. You must go to Tokyo for the purpose of reviving it, blowing once more the bellows, and rekindling the flame to forge those laymen who wish to attain enlightenment."

So my master went to Tokyo. With the help of four gentlemen, whom he had met while he was still a monk at Engakuji and who were his first students, a little temple was built in the village of Negishi at the foot of the slope behind the hill of Ueno. Gradually the little hut became too small for the students who gathered about him. After three years, a new and larger temple was built at Nippori, a suburb of Tokyo. At that time I was a student of sculpture at the Imperial Academy of Art. It was then that I came to my teacher.

The second time I met Soyen Shaku was in this temple, Ryomo-an. It was April 4, the birthday of the Buddha. We were busy with preparations for the festival, especially since we had news that our teacher's teacher was coming. After the celebration and before sundown, we received the Abbot Soyen with his personal attendant. I think the latter was Sogen Asahina, now one of the famous Zen masters of the present day. We were excited to see our teacher, Sokatsu Shaku, with his teacher, Soyen Shaku. We watched them sitting together in the same room; our teacher was seated to one side and his teacher occupied the seat of honor. Our teacher did not lose any dignity in comparison with his teacher, but in his presence certainly he was very humble. We realized that filial piety exists also in Zen. We offered the abbot *sake*, "the hot water of wisdom," because we knew he loved it. It is not unusual in a Zen master to love the "hot water of wisdom," but it is rather grotesque.

As his gift to us, the Abbot displayed his calligraphic art. Seizing the great brush, big as a horse's tail, he flung like lightning four Chinese characters on the eight-foot length of silk canvas: "This very mind is the seat of Zen practice." Later we framed it and hung it above the lintel of the entrance to the meditation hall.

After his calligraphy was completed, I was chosen by the other Zen students to entertain the abbot with a monologue, because they knew that I was always mimicking famous monologists of the day. I was terribly disconcerted at having to present myself before the abbot. "Fancy seeing you here! Have you commenced to carve the Buddha statue?" Certainly he remembered me! My teacher said, "We present him to you today as a monologist." The title of my monologue was "An Acolyte at the Cherry Blossom Festival." The abbot almost died of laughter. "This is the first time I have heard a Zen monologue," he said. I thought to myself, "He thinks I am a longtime Zen student."

# Carve Me a Buddha

*B*uddhism is like the ocean and each monk studies some particular part. I studied primitive Buddhism, Zen, and carving. Zen is also a big ocean, so I studied koans. And in the big ocean of sculpture, I studied Buddhist figures as well as Egyptian and Greek, from nature to nudes. Finally I want back to carving Buddha. One day my teacher asked me: "How many years have you been studying sculpture?" "About six years." "Carve me a Buddha." After fifteen days I brought it to him. "What is this?" he said. He threw it out of the window into a pond! It seemed unkind, but it was not. He meant me to carve a Buddha in myself!

I shall take this opportunity to explain why we practice meditation. We do not practice meditation to digest our food, or to strengthen our stomach muscles, or to find the *chakras* in our spine. We practice meditation to find the highest chakra, which is wisdom.

This mind that cherishes no notion is the mind of *zazen*. I don't like to use "meditation." It always carries with it the idea of something on which you meditate. Meditation does not express the exact meaning of Samadhi or *Dhyana*. There are many degrees of Samadhi—in the first you hold steady your mind movement, but observe its trend; in the second you free your mind movement, but observe its trend as you observe clouds passing through the sky; in the third you are indifferent to its movement; and in the fourth you will really find the ground of Zen practice. These four stages are all the Buddha taught—nothing but this.

The Buddha founded his religion upon Samadhi. His object of zazen was his own mind. He did not practice zazen upon any external object, upon thoughts or words or ideas. He practiced zazen simply upon mind—mind from which had been extracted every thought, every image, every concept. He paid no attention either to the outside or the inside. Perhaps we should say mind exercised zazen upon itself. In true Buddhist zazen, mind by itself is the meditator and is at the same time the object of the meditator's zazen.

Rousing the mind in all circumstances lying outside of yourself so that there is no hindrance is "zen," and "za" means "sitting upon." You are sitting upon the universe in all circumstances. You are the master in every circumstance. This mind in zazen is extended to east, south, west and north. Then you find your mind close to yourself and find that center pervades though the universe. The spatial, timed, three-dimensional mind is molded in such a way, but in zazen the mind is molded in duration, which is a wonderful thing. This duration is not a line or a cord, but is expanding.

When I was a young novice, I meditated all the time. For three months I did nothing but meditation. Young monks coming in would meditate with the students. I was a busy novice; I stood with my back against the wall, meditating, in the evening, in the field. An old custom, the posture of meditation. Put your strength in your stomach. But keep your eyes open or you will be carried out of meditation, and your meditation will be destroyed by a dream. If you go to sleep, better go to bed. If you daydream, better go to a movie. Don't be a movie produced in your meditation—"It is a beautiful world, beautiful woman, beefsteak and onions!" This is not meditation. This is just delusion. You always feel your heart beating in the time of four, and your hand becomes very heavy, and you cannot lift it up any more. You are sunk under the control of nature. Your tongue becomes lazy. You are keeping every view within your mind— sound and vibration—and then you will stand up and suddenly cry in fear. You don't want to go deeper. But this is the usual dividing line. You will go into Samadhi from there. It is not a state. It is a method to separate yourself into outside and inside.

For a long time I asked "Am I alive or dead?" I existed in a pure state and suddenly came up again and saw a new world. It was the old world, but I had separated from it. Meditation is a device, not Buddhism itself. Emptiness is the result of this device, and the student will fall into a trap here. The Buddha warned his disciples one thousand times, "Do not fall into this error."

When I was a novice I made a joke. Practicing meditation many years ago, finally I annihilated everything I could think of. I annihilated all the outside as an illusion; it is illusory, not real, existence. Then I annihilated all the inside as illusory; within and without there is nothing which can be called real. Not only by thinking, but through consciousness I annihilated myself. Then what happened? I found my legs! This is the joke. I had annihilated all the universe, and at the end I, the annihilator, was still sitting there with crossed legs. "At least," I said, "I have found my legs."

The shape of meditation concerns both the physical and the mental shape. To hold the physical shape of meditation, you must recognize that your spine is the central column. Make the straight central column and sit as if your hands were meant to support that column. You must do this in order to meditate. You must not sit on the corner of your hipbone, but straight. You must sit very deep and throw your upper body to the front, closing your hands and throwing your head back to keep your spine from getting tired. First, let your head droop forward; then, throw it back.

Half-close your eyes and look to the front. Do not close your eyes during meditation because later you will find that you will always be disturbed in confused circumstances; your mental shape will be disturbed. Soyen Shaku, my teacher's teacher, practiced his meditation with his eyes wide open, but usually we sit with our eyes half-closed.

You must practice breathing with attention. This attention is the seed of the highest wisdom. "Attention!"—like a soldier. This concentrated mind which is like a diamond is the seed of Prajna, transcendental wisdom. But you do not cultivate it. You have it, but you have forgotten it. You have forgotten your own possession, your usual human mind. You use it like a kitchen knife. It can be a sword of Damocles.

By breathing, you practice this keen mind. The purpose is to learn to use it. You practice this mindfulness of breathing to sharpen your sword of mind, to polish your diamond of mind. To do this, you go through many stages of consciousness, and finally you attain the original mind that is ultimate, intrinsic, transcendental wisdom.

Such is the physical shape of zazen. It is equally important to keep the shape of the mind. In order to keep the shape of the mind, you must keep the shape of the body. If you keep the body straight, then the shape of the mind becomes straight. It is easy to keep the shape of the body, but keeping the shape of the mind is not so easy.

When I practiced meditation in the cross-legged posture and someone came all off a sudden and pushed me and I fell over, he said, "Meditate mindfully!" If you were meditating mindfully, you would be aware and not fall, you would be able to resist the push. Awareness must be there always. This is the first step to attain enlightenment. Not only mind, but the body also. First, you are aware of breathing with your mind; second, you are aware of breathing with your body. Body means not only this body, but the entire universe. So when you breathe in, the entire universe breathes in; when you breathe out, the entire universe breathes out.

Many students think that quiescence is motionlessness of the physical body. What is the position of meditation? People pay fifty dollars for a train ticket to come here and ask me how to hold the spine, how to close the eyes, how to breathe, how to count the breaths, how to take air in through the nostrils. Physical posture is important, of course, but the mental attitude of meditation is more important. They do not ask questions about that.

If you examine your mind, minute by minute, it is like running water. You think of a cigarette, a postcard, giving a gift to the postman, or no letter from your sweetheart. It is the human mind, and you go to bed in tears. Not only entertaining the dream, but becoming a member of this dream. That is the world you know. It is like a merry-go-round. All are raving and screaming, using weapons, swords, guns, and airplanes, killing each other and declaring self-defense. The pandemonium of your dream is just the same. You must control it. The statesmen and the military cannot control it. There is just one who can control it, and that is your own Buddha. If everyone could control his own mind, this merry-go-round, this pandemonium and war would stop.

You have a controlling power, a conscious center. You can live sanely. But if you lose control of that center, you will be insane. If you entertain your mind, you will fall into a bad habit. To cure it, practice meditation. Just look into your mind, look into that parade of your thoughts. Look carefully, hard, and boldly. Then in three, four, five months, it will be cured, and you will see the bottom of the mind that is covered by that pandemonium. When it is cleaned up, you will see the mirror of your consciousness. You will really become a child of God instead of living in a mirage.

To educate people, we make universities and schools, running everyone into a mold like a pattern in a shoe factory. They wear the same clothes and eat the same food. They put on the same hat and the hat is restless. The hat moves up and down because it covers the same muscles of the same mind. In the ancient schools, this was not so, but we have forgotten the method. Without enlightenment, education means nothing; it only creates more and more mind-stuff. It does not teach how to control the mind.

When you meditate upon your original mind, you will find it. When you first practice meditation, your mind will be like Battery Place when the passengers come off the boat from Bear Mountain. We experience this endlessly. In meditation you repeat your memories many times. But after you meditate awhile, you will not find even a mouse passing through your mind. Your mind will be still as a deep ocean, quiet, transparent. You will find your original mind. This is old mind, timeless mind. In deep meditation, the outside vanishes from your sight, and mind is alone in endless space, mind is pervading in multifold directions. It is a timeless mind. In deep meditation, you will realize it.

Mind is in movement. It carries the mind-stuff as waves carry debris: old shoes, dead cats, weeds and sawdust. It is a queer thing, this mind stuff, and you cannot deny its existence. If you are meditating, you have one thought, and a storm begins to brew in your mind. If you clean up this debris in your mind, you will have pure mind movement. Immediately you will make contact with the universe. Gather your thoughts and see the bottom of your mind. From that base, the intrinsic wisdom that is enlightenment will be born.

Sometimes your mind will separate from intention and go along with your content, just as in a dream. In that moment, you go with the stream that flows into infinite space. Everything comes together and then goes away, and you are standing at the crossroads. If your mind is carried away with the current, you are not yet there. You are a conductor, and you are receiving. You know what is going on, but you should not go with it.

Don't let any thought pass without stamping it! Be like an immigration officer. One, two, three! It is said of a haunting ghost that if you call his name, he disappears. So it is with thoughts—they vanish if you become aware of them. It is something like the work of the psychologist today: he must know what thoughts are "eating" his patient. Then he can name them.

If you exterminate mind-stuff, the first mind returns to you. In that moment—ah!—you have renounced the physical home and the mental home, two dead houses.

If you meditate for many years, you will grow strong and well. You will read another's mind directly. You will become physically calm and mentally strong because you will not waste your brain power on notions. Meditation is the best practice to make one's personality strong. Zen students are always calm and healthy-looking because of this practice of zazen. The Zen student meets others as an ox meets a chicken. If you practice meditation for a long time, you will find this out naturally when you cultivate your own position of mind.

Samadhi can be translated as absorption, or a concentration which has a profound meaning. Like a cat watching a rat. When the rat moves, the cat moves too. The rat is also in Samadhi, but when the rat becomes weak and loses his light or when the cat becomes weak, the rat runs away.

Many monks just sit, and sitting is all. When you sit one moment, you are Buddha for one moment. When you sit one hour, you are Buddha for one hour. And when you realize you are a Buddha, you stand up and walk. You are walking! You are eating! You realize you are a Buddha. It is one way to do it and it is a good way. But the trouble is they do not use their brains; they just sit. In the Southern School of Zen, we meditate to concentrate ourselves upon that focus, but meditation is not the main point. To strike that focus is the main point. So we can stand and meditate. We can meditate anywhere; working in the garden, working in the kitchen, we are meditating.

From where does this awareness come, this awareness that I am existing now at this moment and that I know my existence here? First, we find the universal position of our self; second, we localize wisdom; third, we prove *Nirvana*. Then slowly we can free ourselves from bondage. The only point of meditation, Samadhi, is to see directly into wisdom, one's own intrinsic nature—then attain.

When you come to a Zen temple to study Zen, you give away your speaking mind and enter profound silence. Suddenly, in a sharp pinpoint, you find the whole universe within yourself. Awareness is a very important word in Buddhism. The knower is Buddha, the awakened one. This awareness is called *Bodhi*— to awaken.

When I was a young novice, I thought, "Why does the Buddha, who has so marvelous a personality, speak so loudly?" I asked this question of a monk. He said, "Because you are a small person, you think in this way. When you call yourself a wise man, you think you are superior. So when the Buddha says, 'I am the highest, I am the mightiest,' you think him very haughty, very arrogant. But this is merely from your standpoint. The Buddha attained the highest enlightenment, so to him, he and everyone else are one and the same. He doesn't think 'he' or 'you' or 'I'; he thinks there is only one person in the world, not two. It was from that standpoint that he said, 'I am the highest, I am the mightiest.' He makes us high also. You must observe him not from your small standpoint, but from his standpoint." We emphasize self-awakening here. The

Buddha called his awakening that which he "had attained without teaching."

The records show that the Buddha had both Arada Kalama and Udraka Ramaputra as his teachers, and that from them he learned meditation, so it cannot be said that he had no teachers. But when the Buddha attained awakening, he did so by himself.

In the real sense, no awakened Buddhist has had a teacher. I cannot bring you to awakening. You must do it yourself. The Buddha said, "There is no teacher. Self-awakening is the highest teacher." Please remember this.

## Peeling the Skin from My Eye

When I was young, twenty years old, I first entered the
monastery to solve my childish questions. I accepted a
koan from my teacher, who was a disciple of Soyen Shaku, a
famous Zen master. It was: "Before father and mother, what
were you?" Before the atom, before even the creation of the
world, what were you? Zero never produced anything! So what
were you? It struck my brain and I really tried to solve it. I
answered every morning, but he rang his bell as soon as I spoke,
until there was no word. So then he said: "Before father and
mother there was no word. Show me without a word!" I felt as
if I was knocked into the middle of next week!

The masters of the Rinzai school of Zen in China, and later
those in Japan, employed a method of instruction by question
and answer, which is known as "koan observation" or "koan
study." "Koan contemplation" would perhaps be a better

expression for this way of teaching, which is the accepted method in the schools of Rinzai Zen in Japan today. Since this method of training through personal instruction and koan observation is little understood in the West, I shall try to explain briefly its historical development and to show why it continues to be so highly esteemed.

The attainment of what is known as *satori* or Zen understanding is universal, as I have said. No one reaches a final attainment which is different from someone else's. Certainly each starts from his own particular angle, but the reaching-point is the same. The goal of Zen training, even though it transcends ordinary reasoning, concepts, and expressions, has been established for a long time, in fact, since the time of Gautama himself. That state of mind, which is the attainment of the final goal, is, therefore, the measure in the Zen school. By this the Zen master judges and acknowledges the accuracy of the student's answer to a koan just as an official testifies to the validity of a traveler's passport with a visa, or withholds the visa if the passport does not tally with the requirements of the law.

Personal instruction in Zen is termed in Japanese *nisshitsu*, "entering the teacher's room." Sanzen is another term commonly used for the act of entering the teacher's room in order to express the answer to a koan. Originally, questions and answers were sometimes carried on in the presence of the entire group, sometimes in the presence of only a few enlightened disciples, and sometimes in the strictest privacy. Since the teacher was free to conduct this at any time or in any place, the monks of ancient days were wont to carry a small incense box in their sleeves that they might offer incense to the master whenever the occasion presented itself. Later, the teacher's room became the customary place for this personal interview, which was then conducted according to a highly formalized mode of procedure, every detail of which was carefully regulated and prescribed.

Zen in the T'ang Dynasty was at its height. Students did not study Zen merely by taking sanzen, but by practicing it daily. Today, we study Zen as one would learn to swim in a pool, but in Rinzai's time, it was like swimming in the ocean. Both teacher and student expressed Zen at each moment of the day's tasks. The mountain they looked at was a koan; the sky into which they gazed was a koan. Anything and anyone they confronted was a koan. You must take this attitude toward Zen; do not think it is something different from your daily life. Daily life is the real koan. Zen as practiced in sanzen is like learning to swim in a pool.

When you come into the Zen room, try to keep your body and mind in shape. The Zen room is a battlefield. Be trained in zazen! That is your basic training, your boot camp. It is the training in zazen and for daily life. Zen is a very practical religion. My teacher drove me into many corners, but he always left me an avenue of escape. He would lose his temper, but he always left enough room for a little mouse to scamper out! I realized, therefore, his humanity; through such actions I could really peep into his mind. I would smile to myself—"After all, he is a man of Zen!" That is the natural activity of mind; that really cleanses the mind.

When I was a novice at Ryomo-an, my task was to stand at the temple entrance for guests. I thought then I had no time for sanzen; almost always I was barefoot or in cotton *tabi*—my feet always felt the ground. One rainy day I was standing outside in wooden shoes, and I suddenly realized that my wooden shoes didn't feel the wet earth. I thought, "I don't understand Zen, but my wooden shoes understand Zen." My teacher said, "Shigetsu, don't talk so much!"

I was living in a house next to a good restaurant in Tokyo. One day the restaurant keeper, who knew I was a Zen student, came and said, "Mr. Sasaki, you are eating your food in the flavor of the food cooked in our restaurant, and you must certainly pay for that." I could not answer him at once, but I told my teacher and he gave me the answer. The restaurant owner came again and said, "You must pay me!" "Yes," I said. I grabbed many copper coins and threw them on the floor, saying, "Take the sound, but leave the money!"

When I was twenty years old, another monk forced me to drink four glasses of beer. Everything looked different! Little pebbles looked different. I couldn't walk. When I returned to the monastery, all the monks were aghast. I said to my teacher, "When I am enlightened, I will become a great actor, a great storyteller, a great monologist!" He said, "Very good." When I sobered up, I realized what I had said.

Ryomo-an, Sokatsu Shaku's temple at Nippori, had originally been an old farmhouse, but it was renovated and rebuilt under his direction so that it possessed some of the characteristics of Buddhist architecture. It stood far out among the rice fields, and the narrow paths between the paddies formed the only link between the temple grounds and the last streets of this Tokyo suburb situated behind Ueno Hill.

There were two houses in the temple enclosure. The smaller served as the *hojo*, living quarters, of our teacher. Stepping-stones connected the hojo with the other house, a very large building, which contained the temple proper, the student's med-

*Sokatsu at Ryomo-an with students. Sokei-an is at the far right, bottom.*

itation hall, or *zendo*, and the various offices. Just beyond the entrance to the grounds, as is customary in Zen temples, was the large lotus pond, the magnificent white blooms of which came to their full glory in July and August.

At that time the disciples of Sokatsu Shaku were, for the most part, university students and young doctors, with a sprinkling of members of the nobility. The farmhouses of Nippori village were favorite lodging places for the university students, who came from all parts of Japan. The village itself was quiet, but not too far from the city universities, and the households of the farmers afforded both pleasant and inexpensive living.

In rain and snow or in fine weather, at six o'clock in the

morning we students were assembled waiting for the gate of Ryomo-an to open. Quietly we would enter the temple and sit together in the big room which served as our zendo. We would practice meditation after the fashion of the monastery monks. At seven o'clock sanzen began. One by one, we would enter our teacher's room to answer the koan, or Zen question, which he had previously given to each of us. After sanzen we would quietly leave the temple, returning home for breakfast and then going to our nine o'clock classes at school. Sunday passed as other days, except that our *Roshi*, Zen teacher, gave a *teisho*, lecture, which we were all expected to attend.

Five days in each month were devoted to sesshin, a period of intense meditation, when our Roshi held sanzen four times each day. Because of the pressure of their studies, few university students could take part in this monthly sesshin, but many laymen and laywomen participated in it, coming from the city and the surrounding suburbs, and even from the distant northern provinces. It was during the month of July, however, after the summer vacation had begun, that the activities of Ryomo-an reached their height. This was the period of the Great Sesshin, when for an entire month we subjected ourselves to the same severe discipline as that imposed upon the monks of the great headquarters-temples.

I thought of my koan always. When I lit my cigarette, my koan came to my mind; when I drank water, my koan came to my mind. I was keeping my koan always in mind. If merely sitting from morning to evening were enough for enlightenment, then the beggars sitting in the park would be enlightened. To awaken is the important thing.

I was very busy in the monastery and had no time to sit and

meditate. I meditated standing! Working in the kitchen, sweeping the garden, carving images for my teacher, in the bathroom, on the street car, I was always concentrated. When I came into a place for a little while where nobody was, I stretched my mind to my koan and meditated upon it. You must work with your brain upon your problem and boil it down. Then the question becomes very clear. As long as you have any doubt about it, you cannot attain enlightenment.

With my first koan—"Before father and mother, what is your original aspect?"—I came into absorption and then into real existence. This is not mind-stuff or philosophy in the top of the head. So it is wrong to give a koan to one who has no experience of Samadhi. Even though you pass the 1,700 koans, if you have no experience of Samadhi, your experience is not very deep. So you must practice Samadhi.

The beginning of training is to annihilate your mind, and next is to emancipate your mind. Let it go! Stop the mind's movement and let it flow. Stopping it, you can observe the mind's movement. You must practice this every minute; when you talk to people and when you eat food, you do something with your awareness. There is nothing else to Buddhism but to stop your mind movement and watch it flow. You find the secret of this natural movement.

When I received my first koan, I tried to use German philosophy as an instrument to solve it. I was preparing to take an examination to enter the Academy of Art in Tokyo, and as preparation I was studying aesthetics. In his philosophy of the unconscious, Edouard von Hartmann emphasized concrete microcosm. I took this viewpoint to solve the koan, and my answer was "It is like a color which has no color." My teacher threw me out, ringing his bell at me and saying, "We don't deal in likeness or analogies. Bring me the thing itself!" I was dumbfounded.

Then I came back home and took a materialistic view. Before negative and positive and all relative existence that is based upon phenomena, there is just one solid existence, which is colorless. My second answer was: "Transparent," and my teacher rang the bell again. Disappointed, I wandered around Tokyo. Standing before a book shop, I opened a paper and found poetry (from Emerson's "Self Reliance") translated into Japanese. Certainly it opened my eye to an entirely new vista, and later I walked into this avenue and found the gate of Zen.

I struggled hard, gave an answer every morning—but my teacher rang me out! At last, I had nothing more to say. Then my teacher said, "Before father and mother, there was no word. Show me that word!" I could not answer.

Near the monastery, there was a small pond, which took three hours to walk around. On one freezing winter night, I walked around this pond until the break of dawn. I was going around for the third time when I paused, exhausted and absentminded. Suddenly my heart whispered, "This silence is your answer—enter the silence!" I stood still, fearing to think. Then I annihilated all words and stepped into the silence!

Sitting before my teacher, he said, "Penetrate that silence!"—and he rang the bell. But I knew that he had recognized my silence and accepted my answer—"As a man digs and finds wet sand."

Taking Zen is the training of your mind and willpower. Zen is like going to climb up a mountain. The spirit goes hard—then comes to a cliff. In the sanctuary, when the student offers his answer, the master looks at his attitude, he looks into the mind, the decision, that expresses it. The master is looking at the mood—like a boxing blow, not a soft punch! So when you understand the knack of Zen, then your attitude is different and you use it in daily life.

You come to the teacher and the teacher says nothing. When you pass a koan, he nods his head in assent, "Yes." If a teacher wags his mouth, he is not a good teacher. Then your answer shines in your mind. It is Prajna. The highest understanding of the answer becomes the root of all activities.

In sanzen, when I realized entire annihilation, I felt as though I had broken through the bottom of a bucket, and I understood the poetry of the ancient Buddhists describing the bottomless pail holding the full moon. I appreciate it; I have broken through the bottomless pail of my mind.

When you pass the first koan, you will understand this. It is effulgent, boundless, it pervades the entire universe. You must feel this as soon as you grasp the answer. For four days, when I passed that koan, I felt that I was in the sky. My heart was beating for joy. For four days I could hardly sleep. I felt I was walking in the air! Going to art school through the park in the morning, I felt everyone coming my way was myself. Everyone—all were myself! There was no time, no space, and just one enormous body, separating and walking and thinking. I felt I would stay in that condition all my lifetime. Now I have forgotten the world I lived in before that time. It is in oblivion, but I faintly feel I was in a terrible mess of confusion and fear. I remember that it was really sudden enlightenment. If you haven't had any experience like that, you must wait for it in the future. But it is not all of Zen. It is just the entrance of Zen.

When you realize all the universe is yourself, then you have a good answer. With a silent answer, the world of being and non-being come together in the dynamic silence in which something is about to happen and does not. This living presence is in the living present. All answers will be created by the student. If the answer meets with what has been handed down, the teacher may say, "Once the best answer we knew was like this." And you compare the old type of answer—you see it is not so different.

When I answered the koan: "Before father and mother, what was your original aspect?" and got into this "original aspect," I met God and at last destroyed the question which had bothered me for years. This was a very long time ago, this first step, this entrance into Zen Buddhism. I never supplicate the Buddha for my birth in heaven; I know where heaven is.

When I was living in the temple, I did not listen to gossip for many years. I had come to enlighten myself and that is all that I cared for. I did not pay attention to my teacher's criticism, or to the criticism of my friends. I simply went to sanzen with an answer or not. Now, in a Zen temple, if someone asks me what is emptiness, I say, "Come here and I will teach you what is emptiness!"

Now I realize that from morning to evening I am true. There is no false time. Every moment is a true moment. People ask me sometimes, "Sokei-an, you have experienced the transcendental world and you are still there. How do you feel?" I say, "I feel just like this. I got into it in my twenties and I have been there ever since, so I haven't much experiences of the other world."

How did I get into it? Well, I shall tell you the truth. One day I wiped out all notions from my mind. I gave up all desire. I dis-

carded all the words with which I thought, and stayed in quietude. I felt a little queer—as if I were being carried into something, or as if I were touching some power unknown to me. I
had been near it before; I had experienced it several times, but
each time I had shaken my head and run away. This time I
decided not to run away, and *zip!*—I entered. I lost the boundary of my physical body. I had my skin, of course, but my physical body extended to the corners of the world. I walked two,
three, four yards, but I felt I was standing in the center of the
cosmos. I spoke, but my words had lost their meaning. I saw
people coming towards me, but all were the same man. All were
myself! Queer—I had never known this world. I had believed
that I was created, but now I must change my opinion: I was
never created; I was the cosmos; no individual Mr. Sasaki
existed.

I went to my teacher. He looked at me and said, "Tell me
about your new experience, your entering the transcendental
world." Did I answer him? If I spoke, I would come back into
the old world. If I said one word, I would step out of the new
world I had entered. I looked at his face. He smiled at me. He
also did not say a word.

Afterwards I realized that to do this needed strong conceit. I
went back home and told my mother. She looked at me and
said, "I thought you would go crazy and die, but now it seems
you have got somewhere." Now I realized that those ancient
people who left home and stayed in the woods or monasteries,
those fathers who went away from the street corner with the
mountain monks were expecting to get somewhere. I understood that there is some place you can get into and find a new
world.

From the new world, I observed this world. I enjoy this world very much. I enjoy this world in favorable circumstances and in adverse circumstances. I enjoy this world in joy and agony. I have no fear of death. This is an easy world for me. I understand those religious people and their state of mind—what they are doing and what they are looking for.

There is only one key which opens the door into the transcendental world. I can find no single word for it in English, but, using two words, perhaps I can convey the meaning—shining trance. In that clear crystallized trance—*zip!*—you go into the transcendental world. In one moment you get into it, and in one moment your view becomes entirely different. Then you understand why people build churches, and sing hymns, and do queer things. Yes, there is another world.

Immanuel Kant said: "Reality is undemonstrable." We cannot prove it by the five senses. But we say that intellectual intuition proves reality, proves that state, proves the existence of its representatives. When I was young, I thought Immanuel Kant was wonderful. When I grew up and read the Sutras, I found the beginning of Buddhism in this writing. At that time, in Japan and China, students struggled hard to find *reality*; today—only a handful!

For each student of Buddhism, there is always some gate through which he breaks into the main avenue of Buddhism. In true Buddhism, there is no gate that is open to the public, with ushers standing on both sides, smiling and beckoning you to come in, welcoming you. The gate of true Buddhism is always closed. When you knock at the door, no one will answer. You must break in. Otherwise, you will stand on the outside of Buddhism, talking about it, but you yourself will never be admitted to see the beautiful treasures. You will have to listen to someone else who has returned from there tell you about them.

In Zen there is no gate. No one can get in. There is a famous saying in Zen, *"Daido mumon,"* "The Great *Tao* has no gate." The Chinese used this word Tao to mean "Law" or "Dharma." It does not necessarily always mean the Tao of Taoism. Your *mind* is the gate, so you do not need to enter the gate. You are already inside the gate. You don't need to open the door of the gate because there is no door. You don't need to break in. There is nothing to be broken. Just sit down with this Great Mind. The *mind* itself is Tao.

To teach Zen you do not need to talk about it. When you talk about it, you cannot teach Zen. Close your mouth and sit down. You teach Zen in that fashion to everyone. Keep their mouths shut and let them sit down. That is the real attitude of a Zen student. There is nothing to think about. Just sit down with the Great Mind. The *mind* itself is the Great Tao. It is easy to say, but very difficult to have faith in.

I was drafted and soon going to war, and I was going to a town to be physically examined. I had looked up the map. I knew my way and walked a long, long time. Finally, I seemed to remember the place I was in and it looked like the same place as before. A policeman was there. I asked him, "Where am I?" He said, "You have been here three times, walking round and round. I think you are crazy!" No, I knew the way. I think I was in a trance—crazy! I did not know anything at all.

There is a koan: "If you meet a giant *raksha* (dragon) that catches you and flings you around the universe, throwing you into hellfire, at that moment, how do you observe the commandments?" A good koan! Through this koan, you will really grasp the true foundation of the commandments.

I was drafted into the Japanese army and went to Manchuria. I experienced detachment every morning when I was eating breakfast—"last day!" I had just graduated from the art school, had been four years in the temple. I had dreamed of what I could attain. Now I must die on the battlefield as a soldier. I must become dust with the weeds and the blood. I did not suffer. I thought this was a good opportunity to practice my detachment, but I was frightened involuntarily at the sound of bombs. My officer said, "Why hunch your shoulders?" In one week I got over it and I became a brave soldier!

There is a story: A monk was always counting the income and expenses of his temple. He had no time for meditation! *Yama* the king of hell said to his demon messenger, "Go up and tell that monk that his time is exhausted. He must come to hell." The demon went up, located the monk and said, "Your time is up! Come with me to hell!" The monk answered, "Through many incarnations, this is my only opportunity to become a monk. But I was unfortunate because I was always counting money and, therefore, had no time to meditate. Please give me a break. Let me meditate for two days before I go with you." The demon said, "Well, I don't know what my boss will say," but he went down to Yama, who said: "You idiot! If you let him meditate for two days, you will not find him again. Go back and catch him immediately." The demon went back and searched everywhere, but that monk had completely disappeared.

When I was on the battlefield, under the shower of fire, I thought often of this teaching: "My existence is like lightning

*Tomeko Sasaki*

which flashes through the dark air! My life is so short—but original substance exists timelessly. It is like a dream. When I draw my last breath, I will go back to original emptiness. Why should I be afraid of death?" Then I did not hesitate to walk into the shower of fire. At such times, Buddhism gives the strength to pass from darkness into light and to return to darkness.

I was elected to be on the dynamite wagon! Dynamite was good for me when I came to America. I got a job blowing up tree roots with dynamite. There was a little string which carried the fire into that dynamite. I realized then, "This is good training for a Buddhist!" Dynamite is very quick. I called this death my slow torture. But detachment helps me as I watch you go astray. If you ask me which way to go, I will tell you.

I graduated from art school in 1905, but got the actual diploma after my return from Manchuria. In February 1906, I took up Zen again. In May, I married. Sokatsu saddled me with these two things, a wife and this Zen.

# San Francisco, Medford, Seattle

*I*t was due to the wish of the late Master Soyen Shaku that the
Buddha Mind School was brought to North America. When
Soyen was traveling around the world in 1905, he dispatched
Senzaki Nyogen to the West Coast and Suzuki Daisetsu to the
East Coast, entrusting them with the task of spreading the teaching of Buddhism. This was simply an extension of the wish of the
original Buddha Shakyamuni to spread the Dharma to the East.
Senzaki stayed in San Francisco for more than twenty years,
working arduously, and finally, when the time was ripe, a Zen
center was established there. He knows me well for I was with
him while my master was sojourning in Post Street, San Francisco, after the earthquake. Suzuki spread Buddhism to the world
through his English-language writings, which have permitted
scholars everywhere to understand its essential teachings.

In 1906, Sokatsu, following in the footsteps of his teacher,

Soyen, also came to this country, accompanied by myself and others. One day my teacher summoned me and said, "I am going to America. Will you come with me?" I answered, "I should like to go, if my mother will permit me." "I shall speak with your mother about this," he said.

When I was thinking about coming to America, trying to make a decision to become a monk, many, many times I hesitated. "If I do no business to support myself, how will I get donations, how will I live?" I thought I might starve to death! So I worried and could not decide to take the vow of a monk. It is easy to decide how to make money, but it is hard to give up the idea. The hard way is renunciation. "Well, if I go to the riverbank, sit there in hunger, perhaps death will visit me. My relatives will think me crazy. My wife will run away and my children will abuse me." Finally, in my own mind, I made a vow: As Shakyamuni decided before he sat down under the Bodhi tree, I will not give up until I come to the conclusion of my thoughts, my philosophy! That is how I came to Zen.

In September 1906, Sokatsu Shaku sailed for the United States with six disciples, including myself. To get my passport from Japan, I waited a month and was investigated as to my money, occupation, etc. Two men had to sign for me, and the American consul in Tokyo had to examine my visa. On September 8, I landed with Sokatsu and six students in San Francisco. Someone raised a bond of a thousand dollars for a permanent resident visa. A year later it would have been impossible. As several of Sokatsu's former disciples had become students at the University of California, we first settled in Berkeley. We laughed heartily at our Roshi when, at the University Hotel in Berkeley, he used a knife and fork for the first time. We watched his face as a plate piled with corned beef and cabbage was placed before him. His expression was more serious than ever as he struggled to eat this food, which was certainly not the customary food for a monk! This was our first lesson in "When in Rome do as the Romans do."

Sokatsu Shaku had other plans for our future, however. One day he announced that he had bought ten acres of land in Heyward, about two hours by trolley from Oakland. When our group reached there, we found a farmhouse, a barn, an emaciated cow, and ten acres of worn-out land. Sokatsu's eldest disciple, Zuigan Goto, now president of Rinzai University in Kyoto, Japan, had seen in a newspaper an advertisement for the sale of the farm. He had been sent by our teacher to purchase the property from the farmer, who certainly must have had no regrets in parting with it! We had confidence in Zuigan because he was a graduate of the Department of Philosophy of the Imperial University of Tokyo. But the land which he purchased was absolutely exhausted. The cow, also, was exhausted!

Under such conditions we began our lives as farmers. On clear days we worked hard in the fields cultivating strawberries. On rainy days we meditated. Our neighbors made fun of us. There was not a real farmer among us; all were monks, artists, or philosophers. The day finally arrived when Zuigan drove to market the wagon piled with crates of the strawberries we had grown. A market man picked out one of the smallest of our strawberries and cried in a derisive voice, "What do you call this, schoolboys?" "It is a strawberry," we replied. Showing us a strawberry almost the size of his fist, he said: "This is what is called a strawberry! You had better send your produce to the piggery!"

I can hardly describe the conference we held with our teacher that night: our Japanese farming neighbors had advised us that what the land needed was thorough fertilization and real farmers to cultivate it. We realized that the knowledge we had gained from our study of Zen records had not fitted us for such work. The disciple who protested against continuing this futile undertaking was myself. As a result I was temporarily expelled from the group.

I went to San Francisco and entered the California Institute of Art and studied painting under Richard Partington. I carved the wooden doors of his house. The following spring my fellow students came to San Francisco. Abandoning the idea of establishing a monastery at Heyward, Sokatsu Shaku opened a new Zen center in Sutter Street. He accepted my apology for rebelling against his plans, and I resumed my study of Zen.

Again we moved, this time to Geary Street. Zuigan Goto acted as interpreter for our teacher as he was the only one among us who had a sufficient understanding of English. There were in the group at that time about fifty Japanese students and several American ones whose names I cannot recall. Two years passed. Then Sokatsu Shaku was summoned back to Japan by his teacher, Soyen Shaku, but after six months he returned to America.

When Sokatsu, after four years in the United States, was about to return to Japan, he told me: "North America is the place where Buddhism will be spread in the future. You should stay here and familiarize yourself with the attitudes and culture of this land. Be diligent! If in the future no one else appears, the responsibility [for bringing Buddhism to America] will be yours!" Following my teacher's instruction, I wandered all over the United States for more than ten years and finally understood the ways of this country.

I didn't know anything about the immigration law. I came to this country and went and came again and slowly studied the law a little. Then one day on the boat I thought, "I can stay two years in Japan, but if the boat comes three days late, how can I be let in?" So law worries you. When you know the law, you are afraid of your misconduct. But you must know the law. In this modern age how can anyone live safely without knowing the law? When you realize the real source of your *sila* (precepts) and the way of emancipating yourself through your sila, you understand the source of law and you understand the law of your country also. You understand objective law and you also understand subjective law. Objective law is written; subjective law is not written, but it is observed.

When I came to this country, I was surprised at your conception of the physical body. You case your neck to the chin with cardboard, and then button it tight, and to keep this from breaking, you strangle yourself with a tie, button yourself at the wrists, and then more clothes, and stockings, and put shoes on your feet and a hat on your head. Only your face is exposed. You abhor the physical body more than we do, for you think the body is impure because it is flesh, because it is matter, not spirit. When I first arrived, there was a little school which taught us how to behave in this country. The teacher said, "Do not speak to an American lady of anything lower than her chin."

I entered a big empty church in San Francisco and saw a gentleman in a corner meditating! I thought it strange for a foreigner, even though I knew that Americans sometimes practice meditation. But on a Monday! He looked like a businessman. I

The Dancer,
*woodcarving by Sokei-an.*

felt uneasy. Is he in trouble? Is there something wrong with his mind? I dared not ask a question and left quietly in order not to disturb him. When I told this to my teacher, he said that all sentient beings are exactly the same in their need to get clear and that I need not assume this man was in trouble.

When I got here, I knew a good deal of English. I could read the street signs and names very slowly, but that was phonetics. My pronunciation was not correct. Americans speak very quickly. It was impossible to understand them. Once I stopped a man in San Francisco and asked him where was California Street.

"Why, you are in California," he said. I said, "I did not ask you where is California, but where is California Street." "Oh, ask somebody else," he said, "I can't be bothered with you." Even in Japan people think that I do not speak good English. It is because I speak slowly. Those Japanese who come back to Japan speak English very quickly, in the American fashion.

When I came to America, my teacher gave me ten dollars in gold, saying: "This is for an emergency. Use it only at the last moment." I said, "Thank you very much," and used it when I first arrived. The last moment came very quickly! The first day I bought a one dollar watch and destroyed it completely. Then I picked it up and enjoyed it!

When I came to this country as a woodcarver, the studio boss asked me, "Are you good?" I answered, "No, I am poor, but if you use me you will find what I can do." "This is not a school of carving!" and I did not get the job. I was discouraged, but one of my friends said, "This is America. You must say, 'I am the best artist in the world—$75 a week!'"

In San Francisco there was bitter discrimination. If we tried to go to the theater or the movie, the girl at the window looked at our face and said, "You have your own theaters. Go there." Churches? To hear English spoken and to learn English? The churches were worst of all. Now and then with an American friend I could sneak into the theater or movie, but never the church. We were stopped on the step! "You have your own churches! Go there!"

To hear English lectures or to attend lectures at the university was also a problem. Of course if you were enrolled as a student, you could attend—but otherwise, no. To talk English, to practice my English? There was no one. Only Mr. Partington, my art teacher; he was the only one who ever took pains to talk to me in English. At the art school, of course, the students were friendly, yet, deep down, there was a sense of discrimination. My paintings, for instance, were not chosen, when others were sent to Paris to the exhibition.

Yes, there was complete segregation from American life. The Japanese had a large area in San Francisco, about from Third Avenue to Sixth Avenue and about twenty blocks long. There was everything there, and of course we were not confined there, but we seldom left it at night. Except for Mr. Partington, I had no intercourse with any American related to my own status in education and background.

I felt this racial discrimination quite strongly when I came to California. I tried to get on a trolley car—ran after it. It would not stop; then I waited, waved, but the car would not stop for me. I looked around a corner where two ladies were waiting. They got on and I hurried after them, but the car did not wait. It was uncomfortable. I do not blame Americans particularly. Racial prejudice exists everywhere. But there is no racial prejudice in Buddhism. At such a time, I always recalled the line from the Sixth Patriarch: "The flesh of an abbot is not the flesh of a savage, but how can my Buddha nature be discriminated from his?" I think in another century this feeling will not exist anymore. I myself felt it quite strongly when I was twelve years old. I went to a seaport and saw a white sailor for the first time and the sight was very strange.

I had a hard time when I first came to America. I was washing butter plates for a while in some Wild West hotel. When I was in Japan, I was a sculptor, but when I came to America, I realized I couldn't go on, so I gave it up. I changed my art and became a poet. As an artist, I needed many things: for painting—prints, canvases, and brushes; for carving—clay, a big studio and a beautiful model for two dollars an hour! But as a poet I just needed a pencil and a piece of a paper and a corner of my bed. Finally, I couldn't even be sure of always keeping my bed , nor my trunk, nor even a suitcase. So my pen became my standing point, or perhaps it was the paper at the bottom of the pen under the sky that was the wholeness I had to have. But most often I found it on a corner of my bed.

Another year and a half passed. Again, in 1910, Sokatsu Shaku went back to Japan, this time for good, taking his disciples with him. I was the only one left behind. My teacher asked me to stay in this country and study English after he had returned to Japan. So I was left here alone with no one to question and no one to measure my meditation.

Alone in America now, I conceived the idea of going about the United States on foot. In February 1911, I crossed the Shasta Mountains through the snow into Oregon. On the hillside of the Rogue River Valley was the farm of an old friend. He asked me to stay with him for a while and help him in his work. In the daytime we were dynamiting tree stumps and transplanting new trees on the mountains and in the woods of the Rogue River Valley near the town of Medford.

Medford was a little town, mostly living off lumber and farming. Farmers came there and settled, mostly from Michigan. There was a main street about two blocks long, houses, one or two banks, and some barrooms. Everybody wore working clothes; I wore overalls all day and night. There was nothing there—just a hick town. Medford was the only place where I found no discrimination. There was none. Everybody was friendly and nice. They were all working people.

There was a girl, a rich farmer's daughter, and I worked some for her father, and, now and then, I was invited to dinner. I think there was something in his mind. I think he had an idea to have me come there and really work his farm. Yes, I think so. I got a job cleaning a bar. The owner needed a helper to clean the bar and to clean the cuspidors. I did not know the word "cuspidors" when I went there.

I was in overalls all day at the bar, but there was very little work. I could do the cleaning in two hours, so betweentimes I walked the streets in my overalls. Then I had a fight with the bartender and left. But the boss discharged the bartender, and took sides with me. I knew everybody in that town. I worked in a roller rink. Everybody was friendly. No girl objected when I invited her to roller-skate with me. My job was if some girl was alone, lonely, to ask her, and she always was delighted to have her life saved! "Oh, yes, I will dance with you, gladly." No, the boys did not make any objections. Usually the girl, of course, had no boy. I didn't like those machine organs making the music. Very few tunes, and the same ones over and over. So I quit.

Summer came with the month of May. I began again my practice of meditation. Every evening I used to walk along the riverbed to a rock, chiseled by the current during thousands of years. Upon its flat surface I would practice meditation through the night, my dog at my side protecting me from the snakes. The rock is still there.

At five o'clock in the morning when the first train whistled across the valley, I awoke from my meditation. I meditated from the first day of May to the end of September, every night. Without my teacher, it was very hard to measure how deep I went into meditation. First, verbal thinking disappeared; then, natural thinking appeared; and third, my mind was filled with tranquil joy. It was like waking up on a beautiful spring morning, seeing the sunlight pouring through the window, and hearing the song of birds—no trouble in the whole world.

When you give a toy to a baby, such as a toy tiger, the baby has a tendency to do something about it. He pulls its neck off and looks inside. Some men cannot do anything until they understand the mechanics of the mind—a big job! As a philosopher or as a scientist or as an artist, a man may start from one corner and analyze all the corners. In his old age he becomes a monk and dies. I had the tendency when I was a child to pull off the tiger's neck, and now I am peeping inside. If you desire to do this, do it thoroughly!

When I lost my teacher, who went back to Japan, I was left alone in this country. I had no one to follow, and I began to meditate upon the *Five Skandhas,* the aggregated shadows of the mind. It seems to me that the Five Skandhas are the main column of the Buddha's teaching. If we open the first pages of the *Nikayas* or *Agamas,* we find them immediately. I was meditating on them for twelve years, and I understood Zen through contemplation of these Five Skandhas. In the *Agamas,* from the first page you will see these Five Skandhas, and all teachers of the Orient place great emphasis on these Five Skandhas, and all the disciples practice meditation on them. I have read many translations made by European scholars. None of them speak of the Five Skandhas.

To explain keeping the shape of the mind, I will use the Five Skandhas. According to the Five Skandhas, Buddha thought of our physical body as a state of mind. When you read the Agama Sutras, the Sutras that are the oldest in all of Buddhism, on the first page you will find a word, *Rupa.* "Rupa" in Sanskrit is physical appearance, that which we can see with our eyes. The object which we can see is Rupa. Of course sound, smell, taste, and touch are also Rupa, but forms and color relating to our eyes are the first Rupa. When you move your body, you are expressing your mental body with your physical body. Keep your physical body in shape. To us Rupa exists in the outside. We believe it exists objectively in the outside. But if you are enlightened, Rupa is your subjective experience. After the Rupa-Skandha, the second Skandha is *Vedana*, the sense organs. All the sense organs should be kept in shape. To do this I have personally always concentrated attention in the ear, hearing all sounds at once and refusing none. In quietude everyone is disturbed when sounds some from the outside, from elevated trains, horns, and the like. Being disturbed, one cannot meditate. Such a person is distracted because he is refusing those sounds entrance. We do not make any intention to receive such sounds, but we must make complete unity with them.

The third Skandha is *Samjna*, thoughts. This is the main point of the training, the head of the monkey that must be trained in zazen. You cannot refuse thoughts that rise to the shelf of the mind like air bubbles from unconsciousness and semiconsciousness. Nevertheless, such bubbles must burst before they reach the highest state. Let these thoughts come. First, you think about a cigarette, music, beefsteak, a glass of water! You cannot refuse them, but you must not entertain any of these thoughts. Let them come; let them go. Your mind must be like a mirror, reflecting but never holding what it reflects. Thoughts are independent existences. Subjective thoughts belong to you, but objective thoughts belong to the outside. If you entertain them subjectively, your thoughts will disturb the shape of your mind.

Some habit of thought penetrates the consciousness and stays there as a seed in the consciousness, and the consciousness carries it through many, many incarnations. We say, "Do not plant such thoughts in the mind." Though you will not accept it, it will grow naturally unconsciously in our mind. It is like a seedling of ivy in a forest. If you drop one, in fifty years the ivy will cover the entire forest. If you occupy yourself with a thought that is harmful and you entertain that poisonous thought in your mind, it will grow and cover your soul.

The fourth is *Samskara*, the movement of your mind that you cannot control. Samjna is the notion you can control, but Samskara is something deeper. In a dream, a tiger is pursuing you. You are flying, but your wings are so heavy. When you wake up, "Oh!" Samskara.

Samskara is translated into English as confection. Samskara was a cake made with seeds. Samskara is the seed holder. In one English word, it is phenomena. How do you like it if I use your English translation "All confections and cakes are mutable?" All phenomena are mutable. While you look, it changes its face. Everything in this fourth sphere is so fine and so ephemeral. It is like a dewdrop: it shines, then disappears. Or lightning in the sky! It flashes through the mind then disappears. By your own mind, you can hardly grasp it. They are seeds of thoughts, seeds of emotion, seeds of desire, seeds of imagination. Many seeds are gathered there. You feel their quality, and in that feeling they assert their own existence.

Samskara has no words and no figures. Samskara is feeling. It is mood. Essentially, it is emotion. It is always in motion like water, air, or fire. When Samskara moves like any of these moods, you feel that emotion of mind. This is the field of the poet who tries to put emotion into words and always feel more than he can write down. Samskara is a very big world. All things in the sleeping state are in Samskara. Trees and animals are in it; every tree and animal has its characteristic emotion. To keep the shape of your mind, you must keep your mood, your emotion, even. When you kill or lie to yourself, you cannot do it. Once when I was concentrating on Samskara, I went to the beach with a dog. He barked at the wind. I didn't feel anything from it, but *it* felt. All of a sudden I realized what Samskara is.

Usually Zen teaches you to observe mind-stuff, the mind in the seed, as a gardener observes the seed in the wintertime, uncovering the dirt and observing it. There are so many seeds, and the gardener cannot know what will sprout. If you observe the mind carefully, you will find some strange impression latent there for a long time. When you observe it sprouting, suddenly you recognize that the *observer* of this inner phenomena is different from mind-stuff. It is not you. The *observer* of your dream is not you who dream. Who is it? Here you have already touched one important thing. To find the One who has no *name*—it observes you, your mind-stuff, your mind motion. This is the gate to enter the real Dharma. All the records are beautifully written—but they have nothing to do with this Knower.

From the Buddhist standpoint it is not so easy to describe the mind because of its many states. The outside is an extension of mind—we see our "inside" on the "outside." The mind you see on the outside is the activity of your own mind, but if you say it is the extension of my mind, you do not understand very well. Outside is your mind. Outside is I-ness. Someone observes this, but we do not know who. When you dream, consciousness dreams you. In Buddhism there is no isolated consciousness. From this gate, we can see all mind. When a Buddhist gets into his own mind, he is in the avenue of all minds. Through this mind, you can go anywhere. So the Buddhist practices getting into all states of mind through meditation. To embody your own mind is the first practice.

The root, ground, or foundation is *Alaya* consciousness, *Vijnana*. It is bottomless. Do not think it has a bottom. Do not ever think, "That is the bottom. There is God!" The feeling of God is bottomless. There is nothing in the bottom of the mind. This bottomless mind itself is a mirror, receiving impressions of mood and thoughts and of the outside. Keep your mind in shape as you meditate on thoughts, mood, and emotion.

These five terms are the most famous in Buddhism, known by us as the Five Skandhas, the five shadows of consciousness. These five shadows of consciousness are the fundamental delusion of sentient beings. Destroying these five shadows, one enters pure Nirvana. Without these five shadows there is no Buddhism. There is a famous line: "If you observe the Five Skandhas are empty, you will deliver yourself from affliction." Someday you will be annihilated and all the cosmos will appear. Not necessary to destroy this mirror of consciousness. But meditation is consciousness, and you can hide yourself in consciousness. Not necessary to close your eyes, not necessary to escape outside. Then you will find Nirvana. I cannot talk about this. By your practice of meditation and concentration every moment, you must know it. A famous Zen master of China said: "Studying Zen is like an ape peeling an onion. Layers of skin and tears till nothing is left, and the ape says, 'Ah!'"

Emptiness or abstract reality is also illusory; it is not the

awakened state. Almost every Buddhist and student of Zen commits this error. He makes a good practice of meditation, and in
practice he forgets himself in absorption. He comes out from it
thinking he has attained reality. He goes to his teacher with the
good news. "Show me your reality!" says the teacher. The student sits down with closed eyes. The teacher hits him and says,
"Go to bed!" Very few understand the true aim of meditation.
You exhaust yourself in meditation—come out and think you
are enlightened. Why don't you get some whiskey and go to
bed? This is also my attitude. You must follow a real teacher
who has traditional knowledge of meditation. Don't just pick up
anyone from the street corner!

Meditation in the Buddhist sense is not meditating upon
something. When you say you are meditating upon something,
that is different from our practice. We don't care for such meditation. Samadhi is the base of our meditation. European scholars translate this term incorrectly because they do not know
Buddhism. How can they translate it correctly! Actually, the
mind is never absorbed in anything. This phenomenal life is in
the mirage of dreams. Everyone suffers from the flowing, haunting mind. It must be exterminated, like a bad habit. It is like an
old man shaking with palsy.

When you meet someone who always practices Samadhi, you
will feel his fine quality of mind, which isn't noisy, but like a
song, which isn't words, but has definite meaning. If you sit next
to him, without speaking a word, he speaks one million words
to you in the silence. That is the seed that he has cultivated in
his own mind by the practice of Samadhi. I like to sit down side-
by-side with a man who has practiced meditation a long, long
time. You feel his tranquillity of mind. The vibration you feel

from him is entirely different from that radiated by those who have noisy minds. If you wish to be a beautiful man—I don't mean physically, but spiritually—you must keep this small seed of *mind* deep within your consciousness. This is the secret of becoming a beautiful man.

Samadhi, absorption, is sometimes positive and sometimes passive. It is very hard to explain; it is an experience. Many Buddhists misunderstand absorption, so they meditate day and night, close their eyes in mountain caves, and think they have realized absorption. Meditation is only a means to attain this absorption. One who does not have a teacher often falls into this erroneous absorption. True absorption is a Buddhist secret and difficult to explain.

Wisdom is Prajna, our present consciousness, with which we observe, discern everything. When this Samadhi and this Prajna meet in a perpendicular line we call it Dhyana—Zen. It is not really meditation.

When I was in Oregon concentrating on all forms of meditation, I was habituated one summer to falling into unconsciousness—not sleep, but something like sleep—unconscious of conscious mind. It was a hot summer, and I almost passed away. I had the fear that sometime I would not come back. One day I went out with a dog on a mountain. The dog was watching me. I heard the sound of a train, opened my eyes, and saw a body. I said, "According to Buddhism one must one day realize that this body is just a conception." I found my body sitting on a rock with the dog squatting alongside. I heard the whistle of the train and realized that with all this universe I am empty.

This is the first step to Mahayana Buddhism. We do not need to brush all phenomena aside. When you pass a koan, you

*Tomeko, Sokei-an and children while living on an island off Seattle, Washington.*

should realize it. You pass koans just as a donkey passes a fence, but someday you will realize it. Man's conception of emptiness is Zen, but you must destroy that Zen—then you will find yourself with all the universe. That is emptiness, *Shunyata*.

When I left the skating rink, I went to the mountains to dynamite trees. It was all Japanese work, under a Japanese contractor, in the mountains just back of Medford. That was work only for warm weather. When the long autumn and winter came along with snow, there was no work. I came there in the snow and I went away in the snow. From San Francisco, with my wife and first baby, Shintaro, I went to Seattle, Washington.

When I came to Seattle, a policeman asked me who I was. I said, "A mendicant." I was almost arrested. "A professional beggar?" "Yes, I am." My friend said to the policeman, "He is a monk. Mendicant means monk in his country." The policeman looked at me. "Is he a real monk or not?"

A long time ago, I was standing on a wooden bridge on some little island between Seattle and Tacoma, and I was resting my arm on the edge of the bridge. In that moment, I forgot my own eye, ear, and sense perceptions. There was just an immense consciousness, which is like a mirror. I was resting upon it, and I felt that my mind was so large and so old in time that all the sounds I heard were heard by *it*—not by my ear. My soul was so big, it contained the whole universe. It knows who the knower is. This is the knowledge of Tathagata.

I took walking trips through Oregon, Washington, and Montana. I worked in railroad groups then. When I was in Montana, I met a tramp. I asked him, "Where is your country?" "My country? The earth under my feet is my country!"

Near the bank of the Columbia River, there was an old man who had been trying to find gold in the west. He had found some depression where no cold wind strikes in the winter, and he cultivated potatoes there. He lived alone, and once a year a little steamboat came up the river. He visited farmers to sell potatoes he had cultivated in the past year and traded for commodities he needed. He stayed until next spring. I came across him and asked him the reason he did this. He said, "Boy, no one has ever asked me why I want to be alone. I am an old man. I have forgotten how to speak human words." When someone meditates a long time and practices thinking everything without human words, no demon can find a gap through which to pivot him; no *deva* (god) can find a way to offer him flowers to such attainment. He is absolutely in Nirvana, mind and body. He has failed to find a path by which he can come down to the world of men. He has swallowed all the Buddhas in one gulp and there are no sentient beings in the world to be awakened. Many Zen masters take this attitude. Another type of Zen master stands at the crossroads of a city, his face covered with dust and sand, and does everything for the sake of the others. The one at the crossroads, though he does not necessarily understand the truth better, has arrived at this particular understanding. I came to this country, lived in the center of this city, and sacrificed myself to give Zen to you. And if you look at me carefully you will find my face is covered with turd.

I had an arrangement with my wife for me to take care of the children during the winters. Then I was free during the summers. I worked for Mr. Schneider in a picture frame shop. It was closed in the summer. Once I went to the Mojave Desert. It was really quiet there, so quiet that I could hear my heart thumping. I was quite astonished at its noisiness in that silence. I was taking subscriptions for the *Great Northern News*. I visited country subscribers, got them to tell me their stories, and got their subscriptions by promising to write them up in the paper. My second child was born. I did woodcarving and published volumes of poems. I also sent back sketches entitled *A Vagabond in America*.

When I sent my wife and children back to Japan, I was very sad. Behind every bush, I kept seeing the face of my little boy. Everywhere I turned he was there. I could not stand it, could not stay there, but ten . . . twenty days—and then I hopped out from there. I could not stay. It was very hard.

# Living Over an Abyss

A fisherman said
that he went to sea by his bark
over the endless waves.
He lived on the plank thin and plane.
An abyss stretched its darkness
just beneath the plank.
I asked him,
who on Earth knew
that all the thousand worlds
Might perish in a wink? Ha!
Sing, comrade, patting your little bark!
Shall I dance on that plank stamping aloud?
Zephyr has blown the clouds
shining like fish scales.
Tomorrow, there will be a big haul.
You can buy a pink pinafore
for your baby.

From *Amerika yawa*
(Night Talks On America), Tokyo 1927

## Preface

Sokatsu Roshi remained in America for four years, but when
he returned to Japan, I alone was left behind. In order to keep
myself going, I ended up having to sell the sculptures and paint-

*Photo sent to Mary Farkas from*
*Elizabeth Sharp of Sokei-an during*
*his Greenwich Village Days.*

ings from my art studies in exchange for bread. Whenever I had leisure, I would grab my canvas and go out to sketch. I would often be up late kneading my beloved clay, using the people around me as models. However, for painting, time during daylight hours was essential, while sculpture demanded a spacious room and costly materials. Caught between time and money, every day I felt as if I could cry. However, in America they say time is money.

It was at this time I began to devote myself to poetry. A piece of paper, a pen, the corner of a bed, and virtually anywhere would do. Whether it's day or night makes no difference. As for models, there is no need to pay so much per hour; everything in heaven and earth—the outer world, the inner world, and everything in between, the world in which the phenomenal

*Sokei-an*

is none other than the real—all enter into poetry. Pursuing this path, I felt the same reverence as when I knelt before sculptures and paintings. From that time I never strayed from that path— asleep or awake, whenever I had a spare moment, I wrote poetry. The next ten years passed as if they'd been a single day. When magazines arrived from Japan, I'd read the works written by Japanese poets. But these failed to stir me in any way. We lived in different worlds. Our ways of thinking, of seeing, of experiencing had become utterly different. It was sad, but it couldn't be helped. At the same time, I had no wish to make myself feel in sympathy with them. Rather, I was determined to walk on alone, following my own path. I was, in some respects, influenced by American poetry and this created another wide gulf. For these reasons I continued my poetry as a truly solitary poet. Indeed I've been content to do so. There is one more thing here I can't forget to mention. In my poetry is found the influence of Zen.

For several years I led a wandering life, finally reaching the city of New York. My carving tools, cherished from the age of fifteen, provided me with a hand-to-mouth livelihood. On October 1, 1916, I arrived in New York. I went to the Great Northern Hotel. I went first to Yamanaka's and was sent to Mr. Mogi's shop, where I was carving ivory and wood and painting boxes—night work. A sailor slept there, and I had long talks with him.

I had a nervous breakdown once. I came into a hall and saw a box; I thought I would be killed and buried in that box! So I think, "I must expose myself to everyone so they will know me." So I was always in the hall in the doorway! Crazy? Yes, I was!

You grow suspicious . . . A nervous breakdown, for three months or half a year. Once in my life.

I lived first in Washington Square South, several places. Once I lived in a rear room in the Southwest corner of the Square, directly across from Mabel's front windows on Macdougal Street. I had a studio on East 15th Street. Very nice. All the places I lived in New York, I painted and left the paintings in Japan. I was a habitué of Petrillo's old restaurant in Carmine Street, haunt of sculptors, artists, and poets.

Appropriate teaching is very interesting when one gives it, but the one who receives it does not think it is Buddhism. I have written about nine to ten volumes of books—everyone thinks they are naughty stories! I am writing for some Seattle paper in the vernacular and in New York in the vernacular, and they think it is nonsense. If I write something about Buddhism they will not read it.

From *Kane to onna kara mita beikoku oyobi beikokujin* (America and Americans Seen from the View of Money and Women), Tokyo 1921:

Preface

I haven't had much luck with money. So I have some trouble speaking about America from the standpoint of money. On the other hand, I have little more confidence in discussing America from the standpoint of women. That doesn't necessarily mean I've had much luck with women, but then again, it doesn't necessarily mean I've had no luck at all. As I wrote, I noticed I had quite a lot of material on the subject of women, and however much I wrote, there always seemed to be more. I began to feel a kind of self-loathing, realizing that I knew so much about women. . . .

## The Actress Who Became
## A Tram Conductor

It's an odd story about the Latin Quarter, but I'd like to tell you a curious tale. It takes place during the Great European War when nearly all the young men had left the city. At this time, the only men one saw in the streets were either old, ill, or disabled. Or else they were foreigners or enemy aliens. America is truly a great nation and Americans a great people; even in the midst of the war, no one paid the slightest attention if they saw Germans, Austrians, or Hungarians strolling casually on the street.

But to get back to our story, the principal sufferers in all this were those industries that depended on a young labor force, and, needless to say, they had to recruit hordes of young women. The time was early summer, and one heard that old men have a chance for a hot time. Meaning, of course, that if in the beginning of summer, young girls are deprived of their young boyfriends, the law of nature causes steam to be emitted from the heads of old men.

American girls, anyway, tend to be particularly attracted to old men. It's not just that they're being nice to them because they're old. I often saw on a train, a girl come into a car, give a once-over to the passengers on both sides of the aisle, and even though there were plenty of young men near her, without giving them so much as a glance, make a beeline for the old ones. And it doesn't seem to have anything to do with her feeling safe with old men. In fact, they seem to recognize that older men are the most dangerous men of all, not just American old men. Yet they head straight over to sit next to them.

I gradually came to realize that it doesn't matter to them if a man is old, because they think that an old man must have some real money. A shrewd merchant takes advantage of every opportunity, and New York women feel that they can profit from their encounters with old men without any danger to themselves. Old men in America, in turn, are quite fond of young girls. In New York at this time, streetcars were five cents everywhere. It was quite common to see an old man board a streetcar, very heavyset, with what remained of an imposing physique, looking like a pig in formal clothes, or a walking beer barrel. Squeezing himself through the narrow door of the tram, leading with huge stomach, he lumbers precariously from side to side, swaying as he walks. But even with all his trouble walking, he's particular about where he sits.

He looks around at his fellow passengers and tries to seat himself right between a pair of young girls. As soon as he sits, the tram starts to move, and he pretends that he's thrown onto the shoulder of the girl to his left. And taking advantage on the rebound, he falls against the girl to his right. And all this for only five cents! I feel like telling him, "Old man, it's too cheap!"

It's typical of Americans that they find this sort of thing highly amusing. If this happened on a Japanese tram, people would frown disapprovingly. Even so, when I returned to Japan, a young lady told me that such things have been known to occur on trams there too. But in Japan such acts are surreptitious; Americans do such things openly, and this is what gives them their childish charm.

### In the Battle of Love, Making Ones Partner Jealous
### Is the Declaration of War

In order to sound a man's heart, American women sink a lead weight of jealousy deep into his breast. In other words, they try to make him jealous. And just how jealous he becomes determines how deep his love is. A man who gives a woman up when she makes him a little jealous isn't worth marrying. And if he accuses her and flies off the handle because of this, he's not really reliable. On the other hand, a man who is driven to drink by jealousy or becomes violent, like a beast, is similarly unsuitable. All Americans, men and women, like people who will really respond to them when they do something. By contrast, bureaucratic types in Japan, for example, give absolutely no response, even when pushed to the wall. They wouldn't stand a chance in this country!

Naturally, a man who is skilled enough to make the woman jealous in return is popular with American women. If a man has only one girlfriend, then women don't think much of him. In fact, unless he's the kind of man who can juggle thousands of girlfriends, not even one woman will fall for him. This attitude isn't limited to America. I imagine it's the same all over the world. But it seems particularly so in the United States.

If a man is so popular that when he goes out, the seven- and eight-year-old girls from the neighborhood follow him screaming, all the women ask to dance with him, and at an evening tea party, the widows and old ladies try to corner him in conversation. If he's that popular, then the women will pursue him, trying to make him theirs alone, exhausting all their wiles to satisfy their vanity and ambition. But this kind of man is never in the position to be made jealous. He is always making women jealous. The more he does so, the more he's looked up to. Naturally, there are different sorts of popular men, each with different characteristics: there are charming men, stylish men, powerful men, rich men, passionate men. And each of these types appeals to different types of women. But, basically, it's the rich, powerful, or optimistic men who are the most popular in the United States. By rich, of course, I mean someone wealthy; by powerful, someone energetic and active; by optimistic, a good-natured man. These are the types favored by American women. Charming men are favored by widows; stylish men by young girls; passionate men are attractive to women who are sports enthusiasts. But I'm talking about a man among men, a king of men who possesses female slaves in great number. On the other hand, there are those men with just one, or, at most, three sweethearts like a crow with a piece of peacock's feather precariously stuck to the tip of its tail. This is the type of man who is most likely to have women test the limits of his jealousy, the type of man whose capacity for jealously will be plumbed by women.

Colonel Fred was such a man. He has only one girlfriend, whom he had met recently, but he was being mobilized to go to Paris, and just before leaving he had proposed to her that they become engaged. In those days, almost all the women with sweethearts being sent to the front rushed to marry. Fred, too, proposed to his girlfriend that they at least become engaged, expecting that she would gladly accept. But unexpectedly, he was refused. Not only that, but she began to see another man, went out every night to the theater, to dances and hotel dining rooms, just as if she were deliberately flaunting her independence. Though Fred tried to reach her, repeatedly phoning and sending flowers, she steadfastly ignored his attention. Fred was devoured by jealousy.

From *Chinese Poems* by Li Po, translated from Chinese by Sasaki and Maxwell Bodenheim, *The Little Review: A Magazine of the Arts Making No Compromise with the Public Taste*, Vol. IV, No. 2, June 1917:

### "Gently Drunk Woman"

A breeze knelt upon the lotus flowers
And their odor filled a water palace.
I saw a king's daughter
Upon the roof-garden of the water palace.
She was half-drunk and she danced,
Her curling body killing her strength.
She grimaced languidly.
She smiled and drooped over the railing
Around the white, jewel-silenced floor.

### "A Woman Speaks"

The keenest of swords plunges into leaping water
And cannot cut it.
My love for you is like that sword,
But winds around your heart.
After you go, the weeds shrouding my garden gate
Fade, and become the ground of autumn.
But spring slips back your footmarks
Prisoned in the soft ground, about the gate.

"Veil Skirt"
Her skirt of veils is like curling water
Covered with golden nets of frail dust.
How can I drop to the bottom of her heart?
I cannot refuse a thousand cups of green wine.
Her red cheeks sink into me, and make me dead.

I was in emptiness. I really do not know how I managed myself in that empty stage through six, seven years, not only in meditation but in practical daily life. I just took, so to speak, a relaxed attitude like a willow tree. According to the wind it goes to the south, to the north. It is like a cloud on the sky, swept by wind and loitering around the moon. I think I was really a brave man to keep that state for seven years—empty of all desire, all purpose.

Pebbles in the moss,
Fringe the river's edge.
I know not how to rest my oar.
Would that I might moor my boat
Within the dream.

When I was a novice practicing meditation, we meditated for long periods of time every night and day. Once a monk remained in the state of Nirvana for several days. He was so deep in meditation, he did not go to supper. At noon, some days later, the monks went back and found that his body had begun to rot and worms had appeared. The odor of death was present. The monks thought: "Poor monk! He went so deep, he couldn't come back. He must have died in meditation. What shall we do?" The abbot said: "Oh, he's all right. He'll come back tonight." That night the monk's consciousness returned to his body. When the abbot stood before him, the monk struck him down. The teacher said, "You have attained!" The monk said, "From now on, I don't care for all those scraps of paper." The teacher said, "Very good. From now on you can walk the Buddha path."

Many idiots practice this. The monk came back, but he did not attain anything. He had a one-in-a-million chance. "Oh, I was hibernating for a while!"—like a snake or a frog in the mud, sleeping under the earth: "Nirvana is like death!" Not everyone who goes into Nirvana attains it. One must have the wisdom that corresponds to its *reality*. They think that this is the goal of attainment, so they fall into nihilism. They think that life is valueless and not worth living. They lose God, *reality*, and *love*. They also lose their religion. This is also an erroneous conviction. Like the one who comes back and says: "Nirvana is purposelessness! To have an idea of intention in this life is erroneous." So he sits down.

This is not a joke! I was in that state for six years when I first came to New York. I sat in the street, abandoned, without resistance, and a policeman came and picked me up. This type of purposelessness is not the real type that was spoken of by the Buddha. One can fall into it and become a loafer, a tramp, or a hobo and think it is a wonderful religion. Now I know it was an error, but I enjoyed it. I was wrong. At that time, my teacher just looked at me, said nothing, and gave me no advice. While I was sleeping, my friends kept their hands off and let me sleep as long as I could. They were very kind. These errors are test periods for Buddhists.

# Awakening Is My Teacher

"I am the highest, I am the mightiest!
To no Dharmas whatever am I attached.
From all craving am I released.
Self-awakening only I call my teacher."
— Gautama Buddha,
translated by Sokei-an, from *Cat's Yawn*

*T*hrough all the Dharmas you will find yourself. When I was thirty-seven or thirty-eight, for three months I would concentrate on my Samskara, then for three months on my thoughts. The next three months I would concentrate on my "sense perceptions." One day when I was in a shop I saw men outside working on the street, and suddenly I realized the whole universe was mirrored in me, all was in me—all sounds, everything. The hard shell of consciousness cracked, and I realized the size of consciousness. I say the size of consciousness, for usually our conception of size is so small, like a hand. It is like a mirror. The great universe's consciousness covers all; outside and inside is just one existence. When I came back from this great consciousness to this physical body and hit a muscle and jumped, my physical body was not myself. Where was I? It was not I. Three months I was in this concentration.

In 1920 I had a second great experience—I saw a dead horse in Sixth Avenue. I went by and saw the physical details—a dead horse lying on the pavement. Something happened. In that moment, nothing was left in my mind. In August 1920, I sailed for Japan. Sokatsu agreed with the validity of my experience and gave me the seal.

When I finished my Zen, when my teacher sealed my diploma (*inka*) and gave it to me—"Your Zen is over"—I came back to my own quarters and I thought: "This is the end. At the end of twenty years what is this, after all!" I couldn't understand. Of course, this must be Zen; but what is this under the heaven, on the earth? I made a poem in Japanese style.

> I was looking for my own house.
> Many times I came to the gate
> But I forgot my own house;
> I did not get into it.
> And after long traveling
> I returned to my own house,
> And realized my friends, my books
> And the enlightenment which belonged to me
> Were there just as they were there
> When I left the house.

And when I made this poem, I recalled old Li Po's poem. After many years he went back to his home on the Yangtze river. He came into his kitchen, and his wife and his two children had died, but the house was still there, and chickens were still in the garden, and rays of light were still in the kitchen! Nothing had really happened in those many years; but his fingers told him that the wrinkles in his cheeks had become deeper. That was the poem. For a while I did not realize this was complete emancipation.

When I went back to Japan, I wrote furiously, also humorously, about many things. I needed no models—all nature, all human nature was a model. I wrote one thing about a Japanese gentlemen. He came on a train with his kimono tied tight about his waist to save his large bag of money—up here! As he talked he spread his legs—so! His kimono fell—so! Women and children all there! I said of him: "Wealth and sex are separated only by a little sash."

I had many cousins—girls. They said of me that I studied archery and gave it away, studied art and gave it away, that I studied Zen, studied writing, and went to America. After fifteen years I came back to Japan, but I brought back no souvenirs, no jeweled rings. I did go to 14th Street to buy a glass diamond ring, but it was $2.50, too much, too many cousins!

Someone asked me in Seattle: "Sokei-an, you have finished your koans, but you are still meditating. On what? You have no koans." I said: "I am like a soldier at attention. I am meditating on my soul." I am watching my awareness of my soul, so my dream will not take my attention away from my own soul. I am watching and I am still in awareness so I do not speak absentmindedly. I am always on the alert, at attention. I try to be aware, and I struggled for many years before I opened my mouth and gave myself entirely over. Upon this awareness between pseudo-meditation and true awareness, I certainly struggled for many years after I finished my koans, and I am still practicing this.

I had finished my Zen. When you attain the 203 koans, you think you have attained *Dharmakaya*. I thought so too. I said,

"Perhaps I could teach my students Dharmakaya." My teacher said nothing, but he smiled that old smile, and I suddenly realized I didn't know anything about Dharmakaya and must go all over it again. Helpless moment!

You may think you finished Zen a long time ago. I thought so when I completed all my koans, but I now know I did not finish Zen at that time. The real understanding that you conceal in your mind must be clear and perfect.

On September 9, 1922, I returned to America. Back in New York I resumed art repair work with Yamanaka Company. I had met Mr. Mataichi Miya, a member of the firm, about a year after I came to New York. It was Mr. Miya who "discovered" me in the traditional Zen manner.

I went through all the koans and my teacher gave me his acknowledgment. I came to America and was living somewhere in downtown New York. During those years I was in nothingness—*emptiness*. I studied Buddhism from twenty years of age, and when I finished Buddhism at about the age of forty, I had lost everything: my living, my family, my wife, children—all were annihilated! I thought: "What is this? I was looking for this?" My teacher had sent me away—no Buddhism. I went home and sat down dumbfounded for two years—Shunyata, *emptiness*! We smile at *emptiness*, but when we get into it, it is not a joke.

I was walking the streets like a tramp—a hobo! Always I asked myself, "From where did I get this present wisdom? From infinite *emptiness*?" I realized that all was empty. But if so, how did I get this present consciousness? I was stuck there for about six years. Of course, I was working on a koan. "I have emptied out everything from my mind; from where does this awareness come, this awareness that I am existing now at this moment and I know my existence here?"

From where does this consciousness come? From nothing? Simple but deep! For consciousness and nothingness were two things to me, and I couldn't make them one. It was a great question. I took that question into myself, and I was really born in that question. Then—Ah! It was something like this, as if I really turned a cone-shaped flower inside out. "Why, this is Prajna!" And from the center of Prajna, suddenly I saw entire existence. I looked at the ceiling, and this Prajna was like a needle's eye. From this needle-eye, I saw endless vistas. I laughed at myself. Samadhi is the body of Prajna and Prajna is the ability of Samadhi. From the ability of Prajna, Samadhi appears in Prajna. And from the angle of Samadhi, Prajna appears in Samadhi. There is a famous chapter in the *Record of the Sixth Patriarch*. In this chapter he speaks about his foundation of Zen. This is the most simplified speech about Zen. You cannot find such a view of meditation anywhere throughout the scriptures of Buddhism. I at last grasped the Sixth Patriarch's mind! But it is not so easy.

Somehow Samadhi comes first and then Prajna. In my experience Samadhi came first, *emptiness* next, and Prajna came third; again I entered *emptiness*, and then Samadhi and Prajna became one. There is not one way only, but many different ways according to the person. And there is some difference in time. But of course that is not real enlightenment, according to the Sixth Patriarch. Now I would say that Samadhi and Prajna come at the same time.

Prajna is the flash, which comes across your mind, able to recognize the situation in a second of time. Samadhi is like entire darkness, and Prajna is like a light, which elucidates the darkness. In Zen, before the Sixth Patriarch, there were two schools, Northern and Southern. The Northern School of Zen did not place its emphasis on Prajna. These students' life was just endless meditation on absorption; to them the practice of meditation was Buddhism. Without awareness, though you practice meditation for seven years, there is no enlightenment. This awareness is enlightenment. You realize it is like an electric light discovering that it itself is shining. "Oh, that's it!" The awareness that is intrinsic discovers itself.

Really, I finished Buddhism then. I went back to Japan and observed some more koans with my teacher. Face-to-face I proved my experience wasn't erroneous but was all right. Of course I was studying Zen and taking koans since I was twenty years old. But the real enlightenment comes in its season, and then all those koans you have observed blaze like fire, and you really understand what you have been doing.

On October 27, 1926, aged forty-four, I had sailed again for Japan. After I had this third great experience and had written my teacher, he replied: "You have attained Prajna (wisdom) but your Samadhi (absorption) is not quite real. I must see you again." He sent for me to come back seven thousand miles. Rinzai only walked back several miles to resolve this with his teacher. I went back several thousand and manifested my absorption and got my teacher's full recognition. You must meet someone who has this experience, who has experienced it eye-to-eye. I spent months to get this!

Thus, from the Buddha's time, this Samadhi has been handed down from soul-to-soul, eye-to-eye, living together and talking together. For this you must have a true teacher, one who has attained. Of course, when you attain this by yourself—*this* is *that!* That is all. From that day, you can call yourself a torch holder of Buddhism. In the Zen school this torch is not bestowed by the teacher, but the disciple by the power of his enlightenment will take away the torch from the hand of the teacher. So naturally the disciple must be superior to the teacher so the torch will not go out. It does not come in two or three years; it may take twenty. It is not easy, but one who has really attained Sarnadhi knows this absorption.

The iron rule of the Zen school is: "The one whose insight is the same as his teacher's lacks half of the teacher's power. Only one whose insight surpasses his teacher's is worthy to be his heir." This is the measure by which the teacher chooses his inheritor. If a teacher hands down the Dharma to a pupil who is inferior to him, the Dharma will disappear in five hundred years. If a teacher picks a student whose view is the same as his, Buddhism will go down as we watch. In the Zen school we must show some progress to our teacher. We must show him that we have something he doesn't, and we must beat him down. Then the teacher gladly hands us the Dharma. It is never for so-called "love" or "because you have been good to me." No! When a Zen teacher transmits his Dharma, it is a championship fight. The disciple must knock him down, show him his attainment, knowledge, and new information. Zen is still existing because of this iron rule. The female hawk, before copulating with the male, will fly for three days through the sky, and the male cannot overtake her. The one who can overtake in the long pursuit can have her. The Zen master is like the female hawk; the disciple is like the male! You must not forget this law.

If you attain wisdom you will see effulgence. Your wisdom

penetrates all existence realizing the reality behind the phenomena. This is effulgence. I saw the light of my soul and entered it, but my teacher did not acknowledge it when I saw him face-to-face.

There is no torch transmission without looking at each other, no medium, physical or metaphysical. It can only be done face-to-face, eye-to-eye. This way, which is the highest reached by Buddha, is not very easy. Buddha said this eye is the eye of communication, or the highest eye among the physical eyes. This eye I am talking about is a very important part of Buddhism. This eye is the physical eye, the deva eye, the eye of wisdom, the eye of Dharma, and the eye of Buddha. In Buddhism all the theories take this hairpin turn. The physical eye and the Buddha eye are the same.

When a monk asked Rinzai, "What is the first principle?" Rinzai said, "As soon as the seal of the three states of realization is lifted, the fiery brand distinctly appears, and host and guest are distinguishable." This is peculiar to Rinzai. I shall explain, but if you cannot understand, do not blame me. The seal of the three states of realization I have translated from the Chinese characters literally are the seal of the three important pivots. "Seal" in Sanskrit is *mudra*. In Buddhism, the teacher uses a seal to prove and authorize a pupil's attainment. When the Seal has been lifted from that which receives the impression, the fiery brand immediately appears. You must not imagine that this seal is impressed on paper. When Shakyamuni Buddha transmitted his Dharma to Mahakayshapa, he is said to have branded him with the seal of the Buddha Mind, and when I transmit to you the traditional view of a koan, it can be said with my seal I brand you with Shakyamuni's mind. Literally, the Buddha "cast a golden mudra to signify his mind" and handed it down to Mahakashyapa. Everyone believed he cast it in gold and handed it down, that Mahakashyapa later lost it materially. In reality, no material gold or any mudras in any shape are involved—it is mind.

The origin was that when you visit a temple they stamp their seal on paper for you. You take it and bow, then go home. In my temple, the transmission is from my mind to your mind; the seal is in the form of my Buddha Mind, and I am proving your attainment.

This is the first enlightenment. You see these three fundamentals at once. In one second, you see your omnipresent body, your omnipresent consciousness, and you realize your present condition. That is enlightenment. What is this seal? It is the self, just as my staff is the seal, but you do not realize it before you see its impression. You must stamp this staff on your own mind, and it will become the impression. Zen teaches you this. Hibernating yourself in meditation is not Zen!

There are four periods in Zen study. In the first period you realize Samadhi. In the second period you realize wisdom. In the third you realize *emptiness*, and in the fourth you are affirming everything and there is nothing that you can deny in the world. You will affirm from God to bedbug!

On August 14, 1928, the day before I left Tokyo to sail for America, while taking my last sanzen with my teacher, a neighbor pulled my sleeve: "Your name is called—your name!" I scrambled to my feet, minus my robe, snatched up my neighbor's and went forward to receive my teacher's full recognition—my own Zen mastership and my own master name.

My teacher gave me the name Sokei-an because I was always

reading *The Record of the Sixth Patriarch*. I am not so good as the Sixth Patriarch was; but after he attained enlightenment he went to South China, and after I attained enlightenment I came to America. I entered the monastery at twenty, and when my teacher said, "Go where you like and speak what you like," I was forty-seven years old. When I asked my teacher for the money to go back, he answered, "There is no such stupid question in the history of Zen!" So for eight months I worked in a factory, then returned to spend two more years. Keep this sincere faith, and Zen will exist in the world; lose this faith, and Zen will perish from the earth. If you have doubt, do not give up. Find the root of it and get this root out.

My teacher gave me the robe that was my teacher's teacher's. With this I prove the transmission of the torch of Zen. When my teacher granted that I had finished Zen, he ordained me and sent me to New York. Can this torch survive? If not it will expire until the Buddha adventures again.

Every Zen master, when he transmits the Dharma to to his disciple, utters this word: "Guard this!"—like a single flame in stone you must guard it under your sleeve. Once it expires, there is no more teaching. You cannot find it in books; you cannot find it in writing.

Sokatsu and I took a turn in the Garden of Ryomo-an. It was a fine day and we looked at the various flowers in the garden. Then Sokatsu said with a smile, "Shigetsu-san, five hundred years from now I shall be born again to see the condition of this country." I said, "Yes. The universe is like a big furnace. To be reborn is very easy in Zen. Zen is such a religion."

Under high heat gold is melted and even
    stones become liquid.
When the mind is concentrated,
    anything can be accomplished.
                                —Sokatsu Shaku

When I departed from Japan, my teacher said: "Before you return I may perhaps have passed away, but I leave my home here (his villa, not his temple) and my articles of art and the desk where I was in Samadhi, and everything as though I were here. Therefore, when you come back, don't feel that I am gone."

That is our feeling. So, when I come to the image and bow before it, it is not worship of the image. Those who come to the Orient do not understand this. We bow as though the Buddha were here—though it was 2,500 years ago. The Buddha is standing before us.

Do not give your teaching too soon. No Zen heir will give the teaching as soon as he has accepted the canon. When he accepts the canon from the teacher, it is like an infant which has just been given birth by the mother. It is too soon for him to give the teaching. As a monk he may be an old monk, but as a Zen master he is a child. He must wait for a long, long time, usually about eight to ten years. These days, though one finishes the study of koans, his master will not appoint him Zen master. There is no koan to study, so he has finished his Zen, but he does not take the position of teacher, but spends about ten years before he slowly begins to teach.

Because my affinity with North America was truly deep, my

teacher once again sent me across the ocean, in the hope that I could find a place where the seed of Buddhism might sprout in the future. Without regard for my own life, I labored hard and came to penetrate the innermost mind of the people of this land. I told my teacher: "It is still too early to sow Buddhism in this land of North America, but in twenty-five years, the time will be ripe." However, someone should go in advance to break ground, to part the grasses, plow the soil, and wait for rain. On the West Coast, the seed has already been sown; on the East Coast, however, no one has yet come to break ground. There must be someone willing to come for this purpose and bury his bones there.

At that time, there were several persons who sent letters to my teacher urging him to let me return to New York, and he gave me his permission to leave. "I am already old and feeble," he told me. "Go to America in my stead and spread the true teaching of Buddhism. Your responsibility is grave indeed. Take care!" As a sign of the transmission, he gave me a fan that had been used by his late teacher, Soyen Shaku.

My teacher wrote me, "You studied Zen in my monastery many years like one day." Such words are written on the back of a robe. The monk who accepts this robe from the teacher goes around to his brother monks, showing them the robe one by one, goes to the temple and to his relatives and friends. The monks will join their hands and say, "Very well, my dear, it is proved that you are the disciple of so-and-so." In the Orient, no one can say, "I studied Zen in such-and-such monastery and I was ordained a Zen master by such-and-such teacher." No one can make such a bluff. This transmission of Dharma is a very important and very grave matter.

So in my forty-eighth year I had completed my study of Zen. I was ordained as a Zen master in July 1928. Under the guidance of a single teacher, I had passed through the training of Zen from beginning to end. My Roshi authorized me to promulgate Zen, saying, "Your message is for America. Return there!" With the help of friends I came back to New York and began my work. My own mission is to be the first Zen master to bury his bones in this land and to mark this land with the seal of the Buddha's teaching.

> Down to the the old harbor town
> You cross the river tide.
> Slowly . . . the ferry
> Carries you far away home on the brow of the moon.

When a Zen master has made an heir, he lets him go far away. He does not depend upon his heir. It is as a tiger or a lion which lets its child go. That is the end of their relation. "Go—farewell!" There is no more communication between them: "Oh my disciple, I am hungry; send back some potatoes you get from the laymen." It is just as the mother lion drops her cub off the cliff, hoping he will be all right. This is the tradition of the Zen school. But the Zen master does not give the permission of the canon before the disciple is mature and fully understands the teaching.

The Sixth Patriarch waited for fifteen years before he began to teach. Many Zen masters wait for a longer time. Usually they will not start any teaching until someone finds them out, so they hide themselves in obscurity. The more he is hidden, the more effort people must make to discover him. Precious things are always hidden; they are never exposed on a street corner. If you have a diamond, you will not leave it on the corner of your desk. You will certainly keep it somewhere so that a stranger cannot find it. True things try to hide themselves. It is natural. Only

impostors come around with brass bands—"Here I am!" The
true one waits until someone recognizes him. But in today's civilization, what is true in human life is never found.

### "Evening Twilight"

Through the pearl of evening twilight
the fire lotus sifts her petals
before the night.
Her flaming heart falls slowly
into the depths and darkness
of the Earth.
That fathomless silence of darkness
never frightens those falling petals
as she follows her destined way:
But in the glowing heart of the day
something of another world
still lingers at the water's edge.
In the pearl of evening twilight
the lotus hides her heart of fire.

## Footsteps in the Invisible World

*I* brought Buddhism to America. It has no value here now, but America will slowly realize its value and say that Buddhism gives us something that we can certainly use as a base or a foundation for our mind. This effort is like holding the lotus to the rock, hoping it will take root.

How to act? How to create? How to create a little temple such as this one with formless almsgiving! I began my teaching in this country by gathering some people in Central Park. The place does not matter. As the Sixth Patriarch said, "If you understand how to speak, how to act, how to practice, and how to do things in this way, you will not lose the cardinal principle of my sect."

Mr. Miya introduced me to the Orientalia Bookstore on 58th street, and I began a series of lectures there. Attendance averaged ten to fifteen people. I gave lectures once a week, from about April all through the summer of 1928. I met Iwami at Orientalia. He heard lectures and began to be crazy about Zen. Meanwhile Mr. Miya, who had met with my teacher in Japan, had been busy in New York forming a committee, which on April 8, 1928 wrote Sokatsu Shaku, asking him to send his pupil Shigetsu Sasaki to teach an American group here. Mr. Miya's name was signed to this letter and also Dwight Goddard's, the only American on the list.

Dr. Goddard was Iwami's business. He got one of the circulars Goddard was always sending around and wrote to him about the Zen religion. Dr. Goddard was terribly moved that he never knew about Zen Buddhism. Iwami invited him to the Nippon club, and Dr. Goddard came with his wife and ate *sukiyaki* and *sake* until Iwami was anxious that he would die of indigestion. Then Goddard said he would study Zen. He went to Japan and China. He could not wait for a Zen master to come and felt he must go after one.

Sokatsu Shaku replied to the American Committee's letter of invitation, giving me permission to return as a teacher. When I came to America the last time and was staying at Iwami's house for eight months, my teacher wrote me a letter: "Your daily provision is in your Dharma Mind." But I had lost it and had to seek for it again. The word was true—it was in my Dharma Mind. This is the heart of Buddhism. We believe Buddha does not feed us—our link is in our Dharma Mind and not vice versa. Dharma Mind is the first thing that we have to uphold. There is deep significance underlying these words!

The American Committee's first meeting was at Iwami's, on Dyckman Street. It was attended by Cahn and Sanborn and one more man. Then young girls came, Maude Iwami's friends. I lived for eight months at Iwami's, from September 1928 through May 1929. I did no work while at Iwami's. I had some money from him, but I had to send money to my family, about sixty dollars. I spoke of Iwami's jealousy to Maude. I was so mad. She said, "You had better go if you are wise." I moved from Iwami's to West 113th Street, and gave lectures at Fina's house. Then in May 1929, I moved to a Negro's house on West 53rd Street under the El. I had a very nice room and lived there about eight months. I was living under the elevated. If you entertain the noise, you die in half a day! But you have forgotten about it. You are like the man who went to the country and could not bear the noise of the country, and came back to the city at once!

In the history of Zen it is not an unusual thing for a monk to go away from a temple where he has been living for ten, fifteen years. For a Zen master there are three rules: 1. You shall not unpack your outfit—your trunk—for as many years as you live in that temple. 2. You must hang your umbrella hat on the wall. 3. You must keep your straw sandals ready. I have unpacked, but for two years I did not unpack my trunk. There was a big reason. The Buddhist monk must not give himself to two powers: first, the power of gold; second, the power of government. Even though my head will separate from my body, I will not twist my Zen.

When I came to this country in 1928, I was teaching young ladies to meditate for half an hour. And in three days no one came into my place. So five minutes! But that was very long, and I reduced it to one minute, and one young lady fainted! On one occasion I began to teach a young girl who was a disciple of some occultist. The girl went back and reported to him. He said, "Wonderful stuff! Get it out of him—get it out of him!" A wonderful expression, but I felt it was a queer one at the time. So come with your shovels and pickax. Get it out! I will not hinder you. I will be very glad if you can get it out of me.

Iwami had sent a report to Japan, and then I had a letter from my teacher, saying I was no good, had no guts, had done nothing, was a failure, that it was a big mistake to send me to America.

A religious teacher comes into a town like New York, and he tries to get pupils. Then those from China or from Japan who know him whisper! From the Buddhist standpoint we must accept this in silence, must not make any objection, or must say, "I am glad that you have given me an opportunity of paying back my old karma." If people speak of him out loud, he is paying back his old karma. If they keep silent, what can he do! Later, when he has paid all his debts, he can create something. If people talk about you, do not be excited.

I went to Goddard's, in Thetford, Vermont, in the early spring of 1929. I had never seen Goddard, but had corresponded with him. I had been invited there as I was about to leave Iwami. I accepted his invitation.

I recollect something that happened when I visited Dr. Goddard in Vermont. He has three hundred acres, and in the center of them there are big dry woods which have been dead a long time. He said, "I always come beneath this tree and meditate." I asked him, "Then you must know this tree, these woods?" And I hit the big tree—hit it! "Then you must know this tree?" My question did not penetrate his mind. He looked at the sky. "Yes, this has been dead a long time!" I observed that he did not meditate—he would never understand that tree. He had been dead a long time ago. I felt I had made a connection, an association. You cannot observe when the Zen master observes you in that connection.

The first day I was with Dr. Goddard in Thetford he asked me, "How did you come to Buddhism?" "One summer," I told him, "to keep me financially solvent, I took a position in the parcel post office in Tokyo. There were plenty of disturbances from the time I went in at night till one in the morning. Then, from 1:00 to 5:00 AM, we spent our time in discussion. One law student there told me four words—subjective, objective, abstract, concrete. This made me begin to think until I went crazy! What were these words? What did they mean? This made me what I am today." Dr. Goddard said: "Cook my potatoes!" I was very glad of that word! I thought he talked to me in the freedom of Zen.

The next morning he took me to his potato field. One man was working there at four dollars a day. Dr. Goddard said to me, "If you can plow, you can stay as long as you like." I stood there and thought about two hours. Then I said to him, "Dr. Goddard, this ground has no trees. Where there are no trees, Buddhism will not grow. I will go back to the city." He said, "I do not envy anyone who goes back. How will you support yourself?" "I am a woodcarver," I said. He said, "I wish I were a woodcarver!" It sounded like he doubted I was a woodcarver! My interview with Dr. Goddard was very unfortunate. When Dr. Suzuki dies, I will celebrate Suzuki's funeral service in my temple. Suzuki has done a service for Zen.

I was here in this city about ten years hiding myself before Mr. Miya found me. I was associated with him for three years before he said, "I hear you are a Buddhist monk." "No, I am not a monk . . . " So one must wait some time to be discovered. It is a shame to a monk to say, "I am a monk." And it is a greater shame to say, "I am a Zen master." He has to wait until someone discovers that he is a Zen master.

A sage was meditating on a mountain for ten days. Now and then he went down to bring up food. One day a flood obstructed his way, and he went aside from the path and saw many ascetics sitting among the rocks. "Who are you?" he asked. "We are your followers," they said. "We hid ourselves so as not to disturb your meditation." A teacher must have food in his own bowl to feed himself before he can teach anyone else, and then it flows out. It is the rule for all religious teachers.

I have now established my small hermitage at 63 West 70th Street and give lectures to my friends. My daytime is used for work in my usual line of art so that I may have a foundation for my future work. By the members' donations we carry our dreams into the real. So Zen Buddhism is now established in New York. It begins to sprout its buds.

In the Orient we do not have a fixed idea because the enemy does not always come from exactly *there!* When you do any business, do not bring a fixed idea to it. So when I begin anything, I will take the attitude of the Sixth Patriarch. To begin here, the house is the important thing, so I had a house and one chair. And I had an altar and a pebble. At first we worshipped that stone. So I began. We did not have all these chairs then— only an altar and a pebble! I just came in here and took off my hat and sat down on the chair and began to speak Buddhism. That is all.

My original idea was to worship the Buddha's footprint. I carved one. My original idea was to carve two footprints on one board, side by side. There is a beautiful story: Someone found a footprint and said, "It is not the footprint of a man or a deva [a god] or an animal." He followed the footprint, and he came to a wood and found the Buddha. He said: "Who are you? A deva or a man?" The Buddha said, "I am Buddha" (awake).

Here hangs my cowbell, the bell of this cowbell temple. Here by this window I sit. I see who comes in and rings my bell. If I wish to see him, I will ring my cowbell. If not, I will sit quietly and not ring my cowbell.

Today people think they were all sages, saints, arhats (those who are enlightened but not working to instruct others) and ascetics—pure monks who never ate meat or drank wine, that they were like monks living in sacred Tibet. You don't know what the monks living in Tibet are! Actually they were tramps, soldiers and so forth. People who believe in Buddhism fanatically think the Buddha meditated six years, then came out, went to Magadha and gathered 1,250 disciples immediately. Try it!

From "Ananda and Mahakashyapa," translated and collated from the *Tripitika* by Sokei-an, published by the First Zen Buddhism Institute, New York 1931:

Preface

On an evening of December 1930, a small group gathered together in the exhibition room of Yamanaka on Fifth Avenue. There we viewed two figures: Ananda and Mahakashyapa, which my friend, Mr. Mataichi Miya, connoisseur of ancient Chinese art, had brought into this country. Mr. Miya asked me on that evening to write a short sketch of the lives of these two disciples of Shakyamuni Buddha. It was a difficult task to

*Sokei-an*

arrange, in a limited pamphlet, biographies of these two eminent patriarchs of Buddhism because of the rich store of material. I decided to translate, not in detail, but to use those parts of the different Sutras describing these characters, which are well known among Buddhists. I wish also to extend thanks to Mr. Mataichi Miya for giving me the opportunity to do something for the sake of Buddhism, to show my gratitude in at least the measure of "one streak of hair of nine oxen" for the great benevolence of Shakyamuni Buddha, our original teacher.

I take this opportunity of thanking Mr. Kazuo Kawazuchi for his gift to me of the 5,048 volumes of the Chinese version of the

*Tripitaka*, the entire collection of manuscripts of Buddhism. This gift has made this research work possible here in America.

... Ananda had more power in wisdom, but less power in meditation. Therefore, he could not attain enlightenment. One having both powers in equal parts will become enlightened very quickly.

Ananda walked all night and just before dawn, being very much fatigued, he tried to take rest under a tree. Just as his head was about to touch the root of the tree, which was to be his pillow, he suddenly became enlightened! Through his diamond meditation, he rent the mountain of his worldly desires and found himself in possession of the six mystic powers, the three super-attainments, and the eight emancipations and he became an arhat of great strength.

He immediately returned to the gate of Vaibhara, the stone grotto where the five hundred Bhiksus were assembled. He knocked at the gate and cried aloud. Mahakashyapa called, "Who is that knocking at the gate?" "I am Ananda!" "What do you wish?" "I have cleared up all the worldly conceptions of the mind!" Mahakashyapa answered, "I will never open the door for you. If you wish to come in, enter right through the keyhole." Ananda replied, "I will!"

Through his supernatural attainment, he entered through the keyhole into the grotto and bowed down before the feet of Mahakashyapa. Mahakashyapa blessed him, placing his hand upon Ananda's head and said, "All that I have done to you was done to cause you to attain enlightenment. Do not blame me. You proved your enlightenment by yourself, just as by your own hand you should paint a picture in the sky. There is no place to put in the hues. The soul of an arhat is exactly the same. There is no place to stain the mind. Take now your own seat."

Then Mahakashyapa, placing his hand upon Ananda's head, said to him, "The *Dharma-pitaka*, which Buddha requested you to uphold, you must recite to repay the Buddha for his great benevolence. You must tell us all from the beginning, when Buddha first opened his teaching, for all these giant disciples, who were guarding Buddha's Dharma, have all passed into Nirvana. You alone are left and in accord with Buddha's great compassion for all sentient beings, you must recite the *Dharma-pitaka*."

Ananda stood and took a vow before the *Sangha*. Then he seated himself upon the Buddha's lion throne, clasped his hands, and bowed down in the direction of the place where Buddha had entered into Nirvana. With a single mind, he began to recite the Sutras. His opening words were, "Thus have I heard."

"Layman-Seeing-into-One's-Nature-Hard-Practice Shigetsu," inscribed on Vol. 82 of Sokei-an's *Tripitika*:

I, Shigetsu, affirm the present state of reality. I do not attach to the meaning of words. The transmission of mind is without deliberate effort. Vitality is a single branch.

Letters to Various Friends and Students

December 27, 1932

Dear Mr. Goddard,

To come to your question about "Anja Shigetsu," *anja* means the laborer in the temple, one who polishes the rice, or picks up the kindling wood from the mountain, or brings water from the pool, or does all the hard labor for the monks. He is not of the same rank as a monk, but lives in the temple community, observing the same commandments as does the novice.

The Sixth Patriarch of China was an anja. We call him Lo Anja because his lay name was Lo. He succeeded to the torch of Zen from the Fifth Patriarch and went to the southern part of China. While he was concealing his effulgence, he still called himself Lo Anja. I was anja also in the temple of my teacher. Until I was ordained as a Zen master, I called myself Anja Shigetsu. Shigetsu is the name my teacher gave me as a Zen novice. "Shi" is to point out with the finger—"getsu" means moon. "To point out the moon" means a Sutra, because a Sutra points out the moon of the soul, but no one sees a moon. When I was ordained, my teacher said, "After all, that blind finger was a moon."

Sokei-ann [sic] is the name of my hermitage. "Ann" means hermitage. "Sokei" is the name of a place in which the Sixth Patriarch of China was living. There are not many Anjas who have become ordained Zen masters, but there were several in the lineage of the Zen torch bearers. An Anja like myself, holding the reflection of the moon, ordained as Zen master and striving not to lose it, is an omen of the decline of Zen in the Orient—alas!

I am not expecting to do much in America in my lifetime, before the sun of the Dharma of Buddha appears upon the horizon. I will do as much as I can in my lifetime. Think, the translating of the Buddhist scriptures into Chinese, from the beginning to the end, took more than 1,700 years, and that under the mighty power of succeeding Buddhist emperors! We do not know who will die first, but as long as Dr. Suzuki lives, he will do his best and I will be glad if I can do as well as he. I admire Suzuki, because he was the first to strike the bell, transmitting Mahayana Buddhism—yet this is still at dawn.

Sincerely yours,
Anja Shigetsu

New York Post, *Tuesday, January 11, 1938.*

❀

Summer, 1933
[Sokei-an to Ruth F. Everett]

One morning I found a letter in my mailbox. For a little while, I was in a quandary. To see that unfamiliar handwriting on an envelope and that unknown address. But that quandary was ephemeral, and I evolved my memory from that stylish handwriting, and before I opened the envelope I understood the letter is from you. I understand you will visit Japan this fall. I will write an introduction to my teacher that you can carry with you. I believe he is not confined to his bed always.

You ask me about my future plans. I do not plan for the future,

*Ruth Fuller Everett at Enkaguji, 1934.*

but when I get old and my hand trembles and my eye grows dim, I will go west with my one donkey and die in the desert. You said through my busy days that gateless gateway seems part of another existence. That is a good hit. Dr. G. [Dwight Goddard] in these days occasionally make a very good hit. I think he is advancing in Zen baseball. I am very glad I find Buddhist friends . . . These days it throws some music in my loneliness. Here in New York I am simply living among the deaf and mute.

Sincerely yours,

Sokei-an

A lime tree in the corner
again in bud.
I feel it, familiar.
Today, is my heart
seeking its native soil?
Wherefore came I to this land
and wandered so many long years?

New York City                                    April 1, 1932
Dear Sanborn,

"To raise the waves when no wind is blowing," is the attitude of your letter. Sitting upon the peaceful tide, you do not need to see bubbling ripples. You are mischievous—oh, go to inferno! You are like a bee buzzing in my sleeping ear. I have to break my silence in bursting shout like Rinzai.

A lime tree on the corner of the street is shooting its twig forth from the dry bark. Spring is coming. I feel familiar in this street. Seldom I do go out to shine my shoe and talk to the shoe shiner in his little cigarette box at the edge of this street. "Hello," I raise my hand. He raises his brush, answering, "Nice day." In his other hand, he is clutching the lady's ankle.

Two pairs of sisters in ghostly black robes pass through the street whenever I talk to the shoe shiner. He points to them with his black brush, and he winks at me and I wink back at him, but there is no meaning at all between us, and we laugh. I think this attitude of mind is the conclusion of human life and that is enough. I do not wish to search out any meaning in it. We need great space and time, which is unsettled in the corner of grinding philosophy. Truth is after all one of the wayward creations of the human being. Not such a thing exists in the universe. Bah!

Joshu said to the monk, "Have you finished your breakfast?" Monk, "Yes." Joshu, "Then wash your dishes!" Twenty-five years I was seeking Buddhism, but there will not be anything left, not more than washing my dishes after the meal.

"Nonsense." That is the conclusion of the universe. Everybody appreciates that. Man can associate with other animals with that. A writer can tell his story to the other with that. Think—Fanny Hurst—writing what? And Floyd Gibbons—talking! They are the favorites of the multitude, and they have something to strike the other's heart though all unknowingly; but to me it is great nonsense that they have innately. Sanborn, I think you are too serious in your attitude of writing. Don't write any story to the human being. Write it to the great sky.

See those dramas which are composed in Hollywood. They have no value, but they draw many an audience because they have some principle in them to strike men's hearts. That it is what is stated in the words of Joshu, "Have you finished your breakfast? Then wash the dishes." Good-bye Sanborn, this is enough of my nonsense on this day's noon. Struggle with your body like the horse, but do not let your mind know it. Okay!

Shigetsu (Sokei-an)

Dear Shigetsu,
   Living?
   Dead?

Sanborn

Dear Sanborn -
   I am Dead.

Shigetsu

꙰

April 1st, 1932

My Dear Mr. [Alan] Watts,

It seems to me that you are on the track that all Zen students have passed along, but it is very difficult to judge through correspondence whether you are surely on the main track of Zen or not.

Concerning the general idea of Zen. Realizing the Samadhi of universal life is not sufficient. It is very hard to judge the ultimate attainment of Zen without observing the daily life. Unless a close contact is established between teacher and disciple in order to make certain whether attainment is one of mere conception or one is really standing in its center. From my standpoint life must be Zen itself and we do not care much about the making conceptions of it. I am quite sure you are on the way.

Sokei-an

꙰

It is comparatively easy to get enlightenment, but to repay this debt to Buddha's beneficence, the thanks for the milk of the Dharma, is very difficult. I spent from the time I was twenty until I was forty-seven in study. I came to this country to try to repay my debt. I have worked now five years, and what have I done? Can I repay this debt in my lifetime? When you offer something to the temple, I accept this for the Dharma's sake. As you know, I do not spend anything for myself. Bacon and eggs are enough.

There was just one month's rent in the bank, and not many people at my lectures. Today I see six people. At that time, six people was a crowd—and I would say, "Today was very successful!" I was holding on by a hair—"One month more—then I go somewhere else!"

꒳

## Lay Worker Shigetsu's Five Admonitions (Handwritten on the Cover of a Notebook)

1. Don't be sanctimonious 2. Don't be pretentious 3. Don't put on an act 4. Don't be overly ambitious 5. Don't be greedy.

You will be very wise when you realize that the less said about money the better. For there is, after all, little to say. In the East we stand with our bowls extended, in silence. That is all. Let him who feels our need give. In the West are tambourines and shouting—"Give! Give!" Those who feel our need don't need tambourines and shouts. So if you have but one small cake with your tea tonight, you will understand we must pay our debts and have not much to offer our friends, and for this we ask your pardon. "Please understand." And we smile as we say this!

When I first came to New York, for the first three years this was like a house of debating contests. I gave a lecture and then tea. I had to talk at the top of my voice! It was a terrible time. I wish tonight that I might not hear another human word for three thousand years! Now I think my audience has accepted this view—no debate. It is like a Zen school now.

The time has come and one must grow with the time. If one doesn't know this, he can do nothing. A foolish teacher might come to the city and spend twenty thousand dollars for a building to which no one would come. And then he would fail because his expense was too heavy. One must know the time to spend and the time to accept help. In the beginning, you are set-ting the net and cooking your food—one year, two, three. Then, one by one, people will feel the light even though you muffle the light in yourself.

To attain perfect awakening, activities do not help you at all! If you follow an authentic teacher, read the Sutras, and practice according to the true teachings, you can certainly learn something; it is better than sitting in a cave, but you cannot attain perfect awakening by any activity. Therefore activity is a malady. You will find many religious people engaged in activities—and they think these activities are religion! I am often asked by American people, "I have heard that you have organized a religious center." "Yes." "What are your activities?" "What do you mean?" "Well, any social work?" "No, I am not doing anything." "Then how can you call it religion?" To popularize Buddhism is very dangerous. If I popularize my Buddhism here and give dinners and dancing, perhaps I can move into 42nd Street, but Buddhism will be annihilated.

We receive the robe by faith, but the canon we must receive by intuition. I cannot tell you, "Do this, do that!" You must not expect that of any teacher. If you have an idea that if you hang about long enough, Sokei-an will teach you something—if you think that, I will throw this bowl in your face. I had such a student once. If I starve, I will not teach!

# Seventieth Street Stories

*T*he first thing I noticed when I came to this country was the restlessness of your minds. Your clothes are beautiful, your food is delicious, your houses are strong, but your minds are like feathers. The mind must be strengthened. There is no way to strengthen the mind but by sanzen. Even without a penny in your pocket, your mind must be composed. Your mind must have some dynamic force in it; it must be quick, not stupid!

Living here alone, in the morning, while sweeping the floor, sometimes there is a knock on the door. Sometimes the visitors take off their hats, sometimes they have cigars in their mouths— "Hi! I want to know something about Buddhism!" With my broom in hand, I am ready to strike. But of course I do not. Once some crazy minister came to my door and asked, "Is war good or bad?" I was sweeping my floor, and I said, "Tell me, is this broom good or bad?" You have an altar and make sounds.

That is promulgating. Not in our Zen school. We don't need to beat the upper jaw on the lower jaw to make some sound between the lips. When we feed people, we don't call the food by names: "This is such-and-such soup; this is a so-called lamb chop; and this a doughnut." No, we open our mouth and pour into it!

I have a favorite grocery man. At first he greeted me, "Hello Charlie." After a year he said, "Mr. Charlie." The next year it was "Reverend" and now he calls me "Doctor." He has completely dropped the "Charlie." It is quite funny. It was the same when I had a gangster friend in New York. One time he told me, "If you get into trouble, call me and I will help you with my gang."

I gave a little Buddha to a cousin of the janitress on the other side of the street when her husband had no job. He got one awfully good job; then they went out of the city and prospered—they now have an automobile, and their children go to high school. They believe the Buddha brought good luck. So even Mrs. Meyer, my landlady, asked for one.

When I was there in 1930, the little daughter of the janitress was twelve years old, selling lemonade on the sidewalk. While I was living there, she grew up and married and has a child—she should be twenty-three now.

That street has passed through many phases. The dancing girls across the street! On the left side of my house a young lady was living with a baby exposed in the sun all day. I passed and covered her with the top of the pushing car. In the evening one young man would come in—only one. He would bring in goods from the delicatessen—a very faithful young man! One rainy day all the furniture was put on the street—very poor furniture.

The young lady came home and then the young man came home. She said, "You will have to find me another room." "Certainly I will find you another room," he said. She stayed there three days without moving the furniture. The next day the young man did not come back. Then she disappeared. It was the end of her 70th Street life. There was a fire in the next house. They had a long ladder and carried out the dancing girls in negligees. A young fireman was on the ladder. His friend said, "Hurry down!" But a girl had draped herself on his neck. Then the house was raided. During the Depression, a man fell down from a window and died. He was some pimp. There was a fight. A girl said, "Finish him!"

Someone came to my door. I looked into his eyes and said: "You have some notion; what is this all about?" His expression was harsh and dry. "Get out!" He came back because he could not do business with this communism—not true communism, of course. There are many such.

Now, as to desire, or rather, attachment: You buy a beautiful swimming suit in the summertime. You love it because it is of beautiful material and beautiful design, and you are beautiful in it. You wear it all summer through September and into October, and when November comes, you are still wearing it. Finally you catch a cold. This is your punishment for being too much attached to that suit. But it is a beautiful swimming suit, and you look lovely in it, and you march into church wearing it! Yes, I read in the newspaper that some girls wearing swimming suits were refused entrance to a church in Yonkers. And yet on the beach the swimming suit was all right. I was thinking about it then, those young girls in their swimming suits. In Japan, fisherwomen sometimes come to the temple naked—no one thinks anything about it. But from the view of the customs of this country, I think it was not beautiful for the girls to come to church this way. They were too attracted to their figures and suits. And the minister's mind would be distracted. Desire! Everyone talks about desire. People say the idea of Buddhism is to suppress desire. "Don't do this! Don't do that!" There is no such Buddhism in the world. The Buddhist calls this attachment. This incense is very nice, but if you burn it all night, no one can stay here.

A young monk and an old one were traveling on foot and came to a flooded river. On the bank stood a young girl, who was crying bitterly. "Perhaps we could help her," said the old monk. "My mother is dying and I cannot cross the river to get to her," the young girl said. The old monk began to gather up his robes. "Stop crying," he said. "I will carry you across." The young monk was shocked. "Remember the commandment," he said, "You shall not touch a woman to take her in your arms." "Be quiet," said the old monk. "You follow the commandment!" Then he carried her across in his arms and put her down on the other side. "Run," he said, "perhaps you will get to your mother before she dies."

Then he and the young monk went on silently. That evening they came to an inn, and while they were washing their feet the young monk groaned aloud. "What is the matter?" the old monk asked. "I am thinking of your great sin," said the young monk, "We have the commandment—'Do not touch a woman!' And you carried that young girl in your arms across the great river!" "I told you to follow that commandment very carefully," said the old monk, "You have been carrying that girl in your arms all day. I dropped her long ago, on the other shore of the river."

In the *Sutra of Forty-Two Sections,* translated into Chinese in the first century, there is a beautiful story. The Buddha was on the roadside with his disciples and heard a young girl sobbing. Her lover had not come. Her sobbing ceased and this young girl's voice in pure clear tones sang in simple cadence an old folk song of the people:

If I think of him I prove my love is not deep enough.

To think of him proves sometimes I forget him.

If I do not forget him no moment is needed to think of him.

Buddha said, "Listen, that is the teaching of the previous Kasapa Buddha, and it is still surviving in this folk song." We can surmise Buddha's idea as he speaks to all his disciples, "That is the principle of Buddhism." If we attach too much to it, we cannot get it. Your soul you do not forget, of course, but if you search for it, you cannot find it. "Who by searching can find it?" This is a little gem. We understand the Buddha's personality here.

In Japan there is a saying: One punishes the crime, but the man we do not punish. We say we punish the crime of the man, but not his true Buddhahood. This is some talk! We think it is true, but how can you punish the crime without punishing the man? There was a famous judge in my grandfather's time, and a Zen monk committed a crime. The judge said, "Confess! Then I will punish the crime, but not yourself." He confessed more than the judge believed! "Well," said the judge, "If you can take yourself from the crime, you can go home. Abstract your crime and you can go home." The monk stood up to go home. Of course he was a Zen monk! The judge said, "Where is your crime?" "Oh," said the monk, "I left it there in your book. Read it!"

From *Hentai Magaiko* (Thoughts on the Red Light
District), Tokyo 1928:

Demons appear everywhere. And the red lanterns of the demon
district can appear anywhere as well. Behind their natural physical beauty, demons always conceal their fangs and lie in wait for
men.

*Preta* (hungry ghosts) live in hell, among beasts, among men,
and among devas. Those whose karma has been marked by
avarice, cruelty, or miserliness fall into the state of the preta
after death. Because of his karma, he cannot eat food. He thinks
perhaps it is poisonous. Something will happen to him if he eats
it, and he starves to death looking at it. This type of preta lives
in the human world too. Some preta eat fire and are satisfied.
But to eat fire he must throw himself into fire. Some preta have
stomachs swollen like mountains and throats thin as needles so
they cannot eat.

In the stories of preta there are many elements having to do
with food, but one never finds any element of sex. Of course, in
these days when a man is crazy about a woman, we say he is a
sex-preta. But originally there was no sex element. In the next
state, the state of the beast, there will be found the element of
sex, but preta are always connected with food. In Buddhism,
food is before sex. Death, or Yama, is first, food is second, and
sex is third. Some preta metamorphose to engender their own
kind; others conceive babies just as human beings do.

There are two kinds of preta, dignified and undignified. Their
occupation is that of gate guard, follower, or messenger. Some
preta enjoy their lives like devas. Others are tormented like dead
spirits in hell. Though they are enjoying themselves, as preta

they must live with preta who are suffering in Hell. They cannot live together and cooperate to earn their livelihood, so each must live individually. . . . Some preta are visible, some invisible. Sometimes the human mind is possessed by preta and acts like preta. As the invisible preta cannot act by themselves, they come into human minds and possess them. So through human beings, the preta act their malicious way.

When the Buddha gives a sermon, all the Bodhisattvas come and in the back are the eight kinds of supernatural beings: Yakshas—violent malignant beings; Nagas—rain dragons; Gandharvas—heavenly musicians; Ashuras—titanic demons, originally gods, something like Satan; Kinnaras—musicians like the Gandharvas, but of lower rank, sometimes described as having men's bodies and horses' heads; Garuda—a kind of bird; Mahoraggas—dragons like boa constrictors; and Devas—gods. These are the Eight Groups, the lowest adherents of Buddhism. There are also monsters, such as the Kumbhandas, with tub-shaped stomachs. Among them, all five of the Evil Ways are represented. When Buddhism is supported, the eight kinds of demons and the monsters support it first. When I was ordained a Zen master by my teacher, one of my brothers said to me, "Your teacher ordained you a monk, but all the eight groups of demons must ordain you too, otherwise you cannot be a perfect monk." I am expecting them!

Today I spent the whole day seeing Professor Suzuki off after his visit to New York, so I did not have time to make my usual translation. On February 22, 1936, I gave a lecture before the Japan Society of Boston. It seemed to me they did not understand my address: they could not understand which was the tail, which was the head. Judging by the questions after the lecture,

I concluded that the intellegentsia of Boston would not understand what Buddhism is. I wonder if my audience in New York will be able to understand my lecture any better. The tea ceremony is what Americans think Japan is, and when Dr. Suzuki takes seventy-five dollars for a lecture, he must give them that and not Zen.

In my sect of Zen, by training in meditation, through intuition we feel these different bodies—the Dharmakaya, the *Samnbhogakaya*, the *Nirmanakaya*. We don't need to use logical procedure to arrive at this. Sitting interfused with the entire universe we feel it. The tea ceremony comes from this. The tea ceremony is a product of Zen. In my sect, through this ceremony, in quietude we perform this agony. Our teatime is different from yours. Sometimes you don't even drink your tea. You only hold the cup in your hand and chatter, chatter, chatter. Our tea hour is different. We taste our tea, we taste the water—the nearest thing to nothingness. We are realizing Samnbhogakaya. We are one of the moons reflecting on the water.

The tea ceremony cannot be done from a book. We must enjoy all the little things like the water boiling. Where does the water come from, from what spring? The tea—what part of the country is it from? The cup—quite expensive, not from any five-and-ten shop! The cup can be valued at two or three thousand dollars, and you must know the value of the cup. The tea ceremony results in a very high form of etiquette: how to hold the cup, how to take the tea, how to make your expression after you take the tea, how to sit down, how to compose the body, and where to place your mind. Those who make tea must manipulate the equipment with no clatter. And those who pour the tea must do so without all the unnecessary gestures here in American life.

The water should be boiled in an iron pot. Here in America you have no iron pots. You used to have iron tea kettles. I have seen them somewhere in antique shops. Please get me one! An iron pot does something to that water. Otherwise here in America you put the tea leaves in and they are scalded by the hot tea pot. Add a pinch of salt. Make the water boil and do not boil it a long time. Do not pour it on the tea immediately. Let it boil about three or four minutes—a rolling boil. My mother, when she made tea, arranged the tea pot. And then when the water was still almost boiling she poured it from a height. Why? Ask the electrons.

I have tried to transplant this kind of tea party into this country, but so far I have not been very successful. I invite you, and immediately you begin to talk. I cannot change you, I cannot destroy your attitude. When I opened this tea hour—do you remember, Mr. Reber, what happened? Many people separated into groups and—*tshaka - tahak - tahaka - tshak!* Tea party? Tea fight! In the early days, I went into my Zen room for a half hour—there was a couple there on my couch! I understand why Western people are so noisy in the tea hour. They don't know the taste of tea! To them it is hot water! You don't eat beefsteak with tea, nor whiskey with tea, only cakes. But Western people take tea and argue like beefsteak and pork chops! It is very distasteful. I do not bring such things from the Orient to this country. I have brought the Buddha's teaching that Bodhidharma expressed as his own view sitting against the wall for nine years. You must not misunderstand Zen, must not blend Bodhidharma's teaching with other stuff. When you try to express yourself by speech, you have to realize it is not Zen.

I ask you to adopt this Zen tea-hour a little more so you do not get into a broken beehive. I am glad tonight to invite you to my quiet tea hour. Please enjoy it. But you must not expect it to be a social tea hour. I accept my friends for my tea hour, and I feel a little cowardly to talk about this, but I decided to express this by word rather than by intuitive message.

At this tea hour everyone has been silent a long time. No one has anything to say. Do you remember when there were so many arguments? I think at last there is a real Zen school here. It has come more quickly than we could have believed.

## Chaka

I call my cat Chaka—in Sanskrit *chaka* means "this." "This" and "that" are very interesting words in the Zen school. There is something, and then you become aware of it, conscious of it—"Oh! Yes! This is it!" Sometimes in the morning when I am taking my bath, the water is lukewarm, and Chaka walks around the edge of the bathtub and then jumps down into the bath. The water is clear and lukewarm, and at first he does not realize, does not know, whether he is in the water or not. He is not aware of the water. And then after a minute he suddenly realizes that he is in the wet water, becomes aware of it. And then great excitement! He jumps out of the bathtub in great fright. He becomes aware of the water. Our mind is ready, then suddenly we realize—"Oh, yes! So it is!" But Western people, English scholars, think there is something strange about enlightenment—some great catastrophe occurs, some light bursts upon you. This is amateur thinking. You are in this great enlightenment—you are already in Nirvana.

## Miss X - One

The river which gives out the smell of the sea is the river which rises and falls with the tides of the sea. Under the blazing sun of midsummer it is refreshing, but in the cold blowing wind of these last two or three days there is no more zest in the smell of the sea. The wind blew in so suddenly that it swept away overnight all those girl children huddling with shivering flesh on the river's shore.

September is really very near. New York's famous summer heat has already receded. From the whispering leaves of the trees in Astoria Park where I have been coming everyday, I feel that the autumn has come in a night. Scraps of waste paper are rustling over the green grass. Yellow dust is swirling along the unpaved paths. In a little ice cream booth at the corner of a reedy walk, I see not even the shadow of anyone.

I had it in my mind that my broken-down Ford should stop at this corner. I have been driving about in this car all summer. It has a bad brake, and so it came that my broken-down Ford, already at the booth, almost plunged into it.

I honked my horn. "Is no one here?"

"Yes sir!" Behind the counter I saw bobbed fiery hair, a pink and white bathing suit under blue overalls, and lips painted red—the mark of a girl!

"Yes, Meester! I am here. Can I do anything for you?"

"Bring me a bottle of ginger ale and an ice cream cornu-copia—chocolate."

"Yes, Meester!"

She spread a paper napkin in a pasteboard box, put an ice cream cone in one corner and brought it out, carrying the bot-

tle of ginger ale in her other hand. I opened the door of the car
and took the box from the white hands of the girl.

"Are you all alone?"

"Yes, Meester."

"Lonely?"

"No Meester."

"Do you live near here?"

"I come from Hackensack."

"From such a far-away place?"

"But summer is ending now. The summer is gone." She smiled
a lonely smile.

The thing which is called "best" is the only thing in the world.
If there are two things which are "best," neither is the best one.
Using the pasteboard box as a tray, I nibbled away at the ice
cream cone. I treasure this trick—it is a trifling thing, but it has
a value proved from repeated experience. In such circumstances
this trick is really the best trick.

"Do you sell ice cream here every summer?" While nibbling
the cone, I asked this insignificant question because I saw the girl
was lingering, looking for conversation.

"No sir. This is just an experiment for my sister—she makes
frozen sweets."

"Then your sister must be a rich woman."

"Why sir, she owns an ice cream factory on 7th Avenue in
New York, that's all."

Wiping my fingers on the napkin, I put away my "tray" with
some money and returned the box to her.

"You know it is said that many a big thing is kept on ice!"
Certainly I admit that I bungled my joke very badly when I
added: "The change should be a nickel!"

For the girl, searching in her overalls with her right hand, shrugged her shoulders and said: "'A big thing is kept on ice is right!"

"Oh, never mind!"

"Thank you."

I closed the door of the car and put my hand on the wheel. Then I looked back.

"So I cannot see you again, eh?"

"Oh yes, you can. I am here three days longer, then I go to my sister to help her. Come and see me there."

"I shall. It was 7th Avenue, wasn't it? Where?"

"Near the Cotton Club."

"I've heard of that place."

"You know, in Harlem."

"Oh yes! I know."

"Sure you know! Don't you go there often?"

"Why?"

"Don't kid me! You're also kind of a mix, aren't you?"

"Also? Mix? . . . Ah!"

## Miss X - Two

It is said that all love dreams cease to exist in the moonlight sky. This summer, however, in the Catskills, the dream of a moonlight sky ceased to exist! For the last two weeks I have been staying with my cat, Chaka, high up on Oneonta in these Wildcat Mountains. When I yawn, Chaka also yawns. When Chaka yawns, I too yawn. Every day, every night, it does not merely rain—it rains cats and dogs! I jumped out of the fire of New York and jumped into cold water on top of the Catskill Mountains.

When things happen like this, there is neither vacation nor recreation. Every day I have shivered under the heavy blanket wrapped over my heavy topcoat. Every night a hot water bottle is placed in my bed. Every night Chaka comes to sleep with me and curls about my neck. I use him as my muffler.

"It is so unfortunate that I invite you to come here at such a terrible season," Miss X apologized, almost shrinking with fear. "Oh, not at all! This is wonderful!" My lips uttered the words, but I was shrinking with cold.

Perhaps it was in his bewilderment from travel by motor, ferry, and train, that when upon my arrival here I opened the cover of his cat crate, Chaka leaped out from the crate and streaked into the woods! He did not return for three days and three nights. He broke my heart! Perhaps he did not know this was the Catskill Mountains. Perhaps he realized it—that cats will be killed in these mountains! Between downpours, like a ghost he came back from the underbrush near the house. Since then he never goes away, even when I try to drive him away.

Miss X said, "It rains cats, doesn't it?" I have given Chaka some liver—delicious food prohibited for a long time. I am making staring contests with the trees around the house. Of course, I have nothing else to do.

> It is raining in the Catskills.
> It has been raining for a month.
> It rained yesterday.
> It rains today.
> The cold clouds wash out the color of summer weeds.
> The mistress of the house—Miss X Number Two—
> Though she rouges her lips
> Her words are colorless
> In the bungalow enwrapped by deep green leaves,
> A pink blanket enwraps her slender waist

And softly warms her maiden heart
The begonias bloom in the window.
The summer we are awaiting has never come
To the balcony where the rain falls every day.

## Fishing with a Straight Hook

*I* am of the Zen sect. My special profession is to train students of Buddhism by the Zen method. Nowadays, there are many types of Zen teachers. One type, for example, teaches Zen through philosophical discourse; another, through so-called meditation; and still another, directly from soul to soul. My way of teaching is the direct transmission from soul to soul.

There was a fisherman in China who was using a straight hook to fish with for forty years. When someone asked him, "Why don't you use a bent hook?" he replied, "You can catch ordinary fish with a bent hook, but I will catch a great fish with my straight needle." Word of this came to the ear of the Emperor, and he came to see this fool of a fisherman for himself. The Emperor asked the fisherman, "What are you fishing for?" The fisherman replied, "I was fishing for you, Emperor."

This crazy fisherman became one of the great teachers of

China, but he never fished with anything but a straight needle. His word was straight, his thought was straight, and his manner was natural. When a man's eyes are opened, he will know a straight teacher; before that time, his eyes are filled with sand.

If you have no experience of fishing with a straight hook, you cannot understand the story. Simply, I am holding my arms on my breast. Like that fisherman, with my straight needle I fish for you good fishes. I do not circulate letters. I do not advertise. I do not ask you to come. I do not ask you to stay. I do not entertain you. You come and I am living my own life.

If you fish with a straight hook, life is easy and there is no danger of hooking yourself. When you get the truth and let it pass through your wisdom, then you have true religion. We are learning what this enlightenment, attained by the Buddha under the tree of wisdom, is, and what to do with it when we understand what it is. This year, four souls have broken into Buddhism by their own efforts. These four students are my harvest for this year. I did not teach them anything. With their own wisdom and their own attainment, they broke into my wisdom and my attainment. We do not express some logical conclusion in words; we demonstrate our real understanding.

## "The Fishermaiden"

She led him by her charm,
She taught him by affection.
She made a bridge of love,
That he might cross over to the other shore of wisdom.
O Avalokitesvara, you are the most compassionate and
  most benevolent!

Sometimes a man finds out about the Buddha's emancipation, but does not know how to teach it. In Japan, there is a story about a fencing master. A man living in the mountains practiced how to catch fish with a lance in swift streams. Without any mistakes, he lanced the fish and caught it. Some fencing master saw his art and was surprised—"Ah!"—and he asked the man to fence with him. The man accepted: he went to the fencing master's studio and took the master's weapons, and the fencing master was completely beaten by this mere mountain man, so swift! And so were many other fencers. Then the master asked this mountain man to teach his art to others and the fisherman was dumbfounded. He could not teach his art!

So, by accident, someone will find emancipation and be one with the universe and *mind*. And when he tries to convey the idea of emancipation, he cannot convey it. But not so with the Zen student. We know how to convey accurately—we just look at someone and we know!

Many people think the Zen school is only a school of meditation. So they "talk" about *reality* and "take" the attitude of meditation. But they are unable to use such an attitude in action, in active life. The old attitude of quiet meditation is good, of course, and is still kept today in Japan in the Soto school, but the active school is Rinzai Zen. Reality is to be grasped in its most active moment. To use an analogy, the Soto school is something like a musical instrument, the strings of which are loose, so you cannot play a tune, though the sound is deep. The Rinzai school is like an instrument in which the strings are all tight. Just touch the strings, and they make a sound.

This is Rinzai's temple; we do not care a fig for the Sutras.

Zen is Buddhism studied from one's own mind. The whole law is written in your mind, in your body. The key to the mystery of the cosmos is really already in your possession. You must read this first and find the law in yourself. Then you open the records of the ancients and say, "Oh, he says exactly what I think!"

If you go to Japan, you will see Buddhist monks are living, not teaching. And all the anjis are working in the garden, making potatoes. And all the teachers are making themselves warm against the stove. No wonder it looks strange from the outside! People say, "What are they doing?" Seemingly no promulgation of the teaching.

Once I went to a theosophist meeting on 60th Street. One woman said to me, "There is no teaching in the Orient. We theosophists take our source from there and we teach." She was just howling. It almost frightened me. I shrank from her! She was not teaching. I take the Japanese way: put the books away and meditate for three or four years. The Zen student is analyzing his consciousness with his own consciousness, not with the policeman's club or the scales! We use this mind to analyze this mind. We do not use the physical eye, but the innermost eye. I do it by myself. I analyze my own soul with my own soul.

We are not asleep and we do not try to go to heaven without wings. All Zen monks conceal themselves in their rooms in winter trying to find the secret of their own minds. Each is doing his own work while having nothing to talk about. Each looks at the other, knows the other's mind, and smiles. The Zen school is very queer. We are not really teaching Zen. We are finding Zen in our minds, naturally. We say, "Don't you know that it is Zen that you have in your mind?" We do not explain. We do not say Zen is this or Zen is that. Those with Zen minds are not lim-

ited to monks. They are all kinds of people. When we meet—
"Ah, that is Zen!"

There is no English equivalent for what we call this in the East,
but the nearest word is probably "opportunity." We seize an
opportunity and grasp the chance of the moment. Other people
do not recognize it, so they miss it. A good businessman always
grasps the chance to make a good deal in any conversation. In
our tradition, if you have a great opportunity, you must be prepared to grasp it. If you do not, you must complete your education through many reincarnations. Then, when you hear a
"word," you will open your eye. You will listen to the Zen teaching and will have a queer feeling. You will really hear it. You will
possess the Dharma in your mind, and you will attain it.

When there is nothing to talk about and nothing to think
about, it is the true view. Then how do you express it? Rinzai
expressed it with a shout. Tokusau expressed it with a stick.
Baso expressed it in a few words, and Gutei expressed it with a
finger. I think that in sanzen, day by day, the true view becomes
deeper and broader. It is useless if you try to grasp this true view
by discourse, by reading or by thinking. It cannot be attained.
If you wish to grasp the true view, you had better try immediately in this moment. Otherwise, you must practice zazen for a
long time.

Isan, the teacher, and Kyozan, the disciple, were picking tea
all day long in the tea garden. Isan was picking on one side of
the six- or seven-foot tea trees, and Kyozan was picking on the
other, squatting on the ground. Isan said, "I have heard your
voice all day long, but I haven't seen your body." All of a sudden Kyozan became quiet. He didn't pick tea, he didn't speak,
he just sat silent. As Isan was on one side and Kyozan on the

other, Isan didn't know what Kyozan was doing, sheltered by the tea trees. But Isan understood what Kyozan was doing; he understood Kyozan's answer to his question. At that time Kyozan's body wasn't very small; at that time Kyozan's body was huge, exactly the same size as the universe. Isan understood. Of course Isan would understand. Isan said, "I have seen your body, but I haven't seen how you use it." Then Kyozan shook the tea tree. That was his answer. In such a way Zen was handled between them.

This is the Ikyo school—Isan and his disciple Kyozan. They handled Zen differently. Isan and Kyozan handled Zen like a conversation between father and child. According to the customs and minds of Americans, I use this Ikyo school style of teaching more or less. You must understand that my sanzen is not exactly like that of the Rinzai school. I take my students as my children and I am their father, though this really should not be my attitude as a disciple of the Rinzai school.

A monk asked Baso, "What is pure Dharmakaya?" Baso said, "A dung scraper." I cannot give such an answer to young American ladies! If a young lady got such an answer, she would just perish from the group! That proves impure meditation—no Dharmakaya in it.

There are varieties of attitudes of mind. When the Buddha was teaching his disciples, he described them as the hard mind, the sharp mind, the mind of a horse, the mind of an ox, the mind of a driver. But the Buddhist should possess a pliant, soft mind; soft like air, pliant as the weeping willow: this is the best attitude of mind. Under the deep snow the branches of a pine tree are crushed with the weight of snow, but the willow trees are never crushed because they have that pliancy.

It is very queer that a Buddhist monk should speak of strategy, but strategy has many things which apply to daily life. The Buddhist strategy is to win without fighting. The poorest strategy is to attack the enemy's castle or the strategic point of the enemy. To attack the weak point is best. And best of all is to win a war without fighting.

There was a famous swordsman named Bokuden, who never used the sword, but used the rib of a fan to defend himself. If anyone would attack him, the enemy's sword would be poised upon the rod of wood. He understood the knack of the soft mind! Once he was traveling through the southern part of Japan by boat from one coast to another. In those days there were no big boats—just sailing boats with about one hundred passengers. He was an old man then, taking his seat in a corner of the boat, quiet and silent. In this same boat were many samurai, fierce and proud-hearted warriors, taking up most of the places in the boat, giving commands to the captain, who was just a fisherman managing those boats, and abusing him with sharp words. All the passengers in the boat disliked those warriors.

Among them was one samurai who looked most abominable. He thought he was the best swordsman in the country. He saw the old man sitting mutely in the corner of the boat, and he kept his eye on the old fellow. "Though he has a sword in his hand, at the worst how could he know how to use the sword!" He approached the old man and kicked his sword. In ancient days, if a samurai walked the street and the scabbard of his sword was just touched and made a clatter, he would make combat.

The old man accepted the insult in silence as though he were a coward. And this proud young samurai said, "Look at the old man! Look at the coward! Stand up, old man, and make a duel!" The old man gave the samurai a queer look. The passengers thought, "Poor old man! How could he! He will be killed, but no one can stop it." They were frightened, thinking, "They will draw their swords in the middle of the boat and begin to fight!" And all the other samurai were clapping their hands and crying, "Old man, stand up! You look like somebody! What is your school of fighting?" It was the school of the moon on the water, or snow on the willow tree, and he used his sword according to that school.

The old man said, "My school is very peculiar and very obscure, but I studied swordsmanship under a teacher who taught me how to win a battle without using a hand." The swordsman smiled mockingly. "Oh? We have never heard of that school—how to win a battle without using your hand! Well, old man, please show us your famous style of fighting!" The old man looked around and realized it was the time of the flowing tide. The tide was coming in slowly.

"Well, if you, young samurai, wish to see my trick, I am very proud of it. But this place is very narrow and the many passengers who are not samurai—I fear my sword will cut into their flesh. If you please, young samurai, go onto that islet and I will meet you there." The young samurai said, "O sailor, send this boat to that islet!" When it reached the islet, the young samurai jumped out, tucked up his sleeves, and said, "Come on, old man!" The old man whispered to the sailor, "Push off!" "Coward!" cried the young samurai. But the tide came in and the old man said: "Surrender! This is my trick of winning the battle without using the hand." He understood strategy more than the swordsman. Everyone would call him a coward, but from the true strategic view it is not cowardice. He saved the samurai's and passengers' lives and won the war!

He took the young samurai back on the boat. "I understand your viewpoint," said the young man. "What is your name?" "My name is Bokuden." The young man turned pale and worshipped him.

In the temple, the monk watches the novice. The novice must practice meditation for three or four months and experience Samadhi before he can be given a koan. A student will come into my room, and I will give him the koan "before father and mother, what were you?" The novice will concentrate himself into the koan with intense, deep Samadhi. There are two kinds of Samadhi. The student first enters the relaxed and dreamy state that is like sleep until he gathers in all the streams of mind. The student then becomes tense, gathering the strength of his body and mind and becomes like steel.

To give a koan to people who have no experience of Samadhi is useless. Zen is not for them. You must be able to concentrate, absorb the question by this power—not by the mind. Then you come to the teacher's room and give the answer clearly. If you are wrong, it is "No." But if you come, cross your legs and chatter, I will throw you out.

So when you take sanzen, I will say, "Show it to me! I have listened to your words, and I understand your abstract theory. But I come from Missouri, you've got to show it to me." From morning to evening you do not know that all these refuges are in your consciousness. See if you cannot see the Buddha. In the Zen room, your check or paper money is of no use. You have to pay in real cash. You must grasp *reality* itself. You have to use Dharmakaya cash. Mysterious, isn't it?

When you realize this state, you can actualize it and practice it. I know whether your attainment is true or premature or false. That is sanzen. It does not take five or ten minutes. You appear before me and I decide. There is no moment, but you sit down and talk, talk, talk. Your lips move, move, move. A poor Zen student! If you were studying in an authentic Zen temple, you would be thrown out. But this is America, so I accept your awkward way. Someone must begin and someone must nurse you. But don't think this is the way we have practiced in our Zen temples in Japan. You think this is only practice in sanzen. You don't know that it is the practice of daily life. Without knowing the law of actualization, how can you live?

Please do not think that Sokei-an is losing his temper if he shouts at you when you do not pass your koan in three or six months. Do not take a personal view of sanzen. There is no person present.

I realize that in each koan you take, you will stick to one little notion—like syrup in a jar. You are in it, and you struggle. Finally, like a fly come to the edge of the jar, licking its legs, I give you another koan, and you drop in again and say, "Good day, syrup!" In the beginning your enlightenment is so weak that I must guard it as a window pane, wiping it. If you are not here for three, four days, your mind is so smeared that I must wash you all over again as a mother her child. And in another three or four days, you are all dirty again when you should be like clear glass.

Till you find out that filth is not the real attitude of mind, I will wipe you. Someday you will find that clear mirror, and you will come into my room with it. I will look at you with respect, and you will know who Sokei-an is. This is not so hard. Just wipe it all off and come in clean. I will look at you, you will look at me, and you will understand what Buddhism is.

You would say that when one takes sanzen from Sasaki, he deprives you of all words by ringing his bell. I give you a question: "Before father and mother, what were you?" And you bring me an answer. I say, "No, no." You become silent, and in that moment how can you prove you have been enlightened? Queer, isn't it? It is very important here whether you go to an ignorant teacher or to an experienced teacher.

I receive you in Zen and I listen to your answers, but I never teach you a thing. These five years I have had Zen contact, but I just listen to your answers and say "yes" or "no." There is nothing to teach. Everything is in your own mind. I cannot eat for you; it does not nourish your body. Your coat on my shoulders does not keep you warm. So in the Zen school the teacher cannot help the student. I cannot give you anything. You must bring more answers until we agree with one another. No reason you have to stick with me. No reason you have to be a student. You must make your own effort and make your agreement with your teacher. In other sects your attainment is Buddha's, but in this sect it is within.

We must watch the guideposts on the corners. All those koans are milestones. You observe one koan and come to a milestone. You walk on and come to another, and you are still a long way from the imperial city! And you say, "Well, I am working on a koan for three months, and I am tired of it!"

A Zen master must get to the bottom of the student's mind. Some people think his method is crude. I have been criticized this way. "Sokei-an is very crude!" Then I become very kind, but I do not give good Zen. If you will accept my crudeness, I will give you good Zen. Kind! Kind! At the time of the transmission of Dharma, kindness is not important.

If you come to sanzen, cross your legs, and chatter, I should throw water in your face! I am in America so I do not, because you do not understand. In ancient days, the giant disciples handled Zen in such a way. But today a student announces, "I will stay two years here, though you throw me out of the window!" Then all of a sudden, he changes his mind and goes away without speaking a word to me, vanishes like vapor. Of course, from the beginning such a one was not sincere.

A student answers me. The answer is fine. But I try once more. The next day he takes off his overcoat and shows me his underwear. No! I strip him like a monkey stripping an onion. Then he will realize.

At this time, I cannot take the Oriental attitude toward my disciples in this country because this is just the dawn before true discipline begins. When I come to this country again in the next incarnation, it will be different! Then the teacher will show and hold the true Oriental attitude, and the disciple will promulgate the teacher's attitude. In olden times, the etiquette in approaching a master was quite different. Today a student may come to the temple to meet a Zen master. He may spend a year or two without passing a koan, and then he will go home and read some books—perhaps write a book himself—and become a famous scholar! Another will meditate in a corner and think, "Oh, I am in touch with the White Brotherhood in Tibet—wonderful!" And he will spring from his seat and write a book, claiming to be a great master.

A Zen teacher does not write books; he teaches eye-to-eye. In the Orient, when one gets this transmission, it is never from books, but from the Zen master face-to-face, heart-to-heart. Then he may be permitted by his teacher to transmit this to the younger generation. But many students cherish their erroneous conception and think it is enlightenment.

I am going to teach Buddhism to a Chinese gambler. I wonder how! You do not need to speak so much, but you have to devise many entrances. But without original ground, how can you devise any gates? And if your teacher has not the original ground, how can he devise any gates? It is ridiculous. It is as if a five-year-old child should say, "Papa, tomorrow I shall earn one million dollars, and I will give it to you as I promised!"

When you teach religion to a woman, you cannot say, "Come on!" The woman would run away. You must make the gate. And to men students, you must make a different gate. True men shout at one another. And for women and children and old men, there must be other gates through which the teacher will go out to teach them.

A long time ago someone came to my house with a manuscript and said, "I came from China." I said, "What is your name?" He said, "Roshi." I said, "What are you?" He said, "A Zen master." I said, "Oh? How do you teach Zen?" He did not think this question very important. "Oh, by lectures and such." If you teach Zen by lectures, you can pick fish from tree tops. I said, "Can you speak Chinese?" He said, "Oh, I am not Chinese!" He was Hindu.

It is not so easy to find a Zen master. If a Zen master can teach Zen by lectures, a boxer can teach boxing by correspondence. If you wish to study Zen, come to me and I will look in your eyes and find whether you know Zen or not.

I try to give you one of the teachings, and I give you candy. You take that chocolate and come again. I speak a little more about Buddhism to you, and you start to run away. I give you more chocolate. The next time I talk to you a little more about Buddhism. Then I do not give you chocolate, and you are angry and try to disrupt my temple. In Japan, often the mother chews rice in her mouth and feeds her baby. Not quite sanitary, but it is the old-fashioned way. And the teaching of Zen is exactly like that—mouth-to-mouth, face-to-face! We will not teach one hundred percent, but we will teach eighty. Twenty percent you must work for! In the beginning I will hold your hand and teach you to walk—like a baby. Then I will take away my hand, and the baby will fall down. Again I will give my hand, and the baby will take three, four steps; take my hand away and the baby will fall. But try again and again, and at last the baby will walk. I teach you that corner and that corner, and you cannot find the center. If you are smart, you will find the center, but you don't.

Sometimes you will meet religious people on the street. I met one near here who walked the street sweeping his skirts, and his face was shining. It was as if he had come out of the hospital in that little nightgown to walk the street. He was still in a religious hospital! The more they strive for Buddha, the more serious the illness becomes. How can they attain pure awakening? Buddhism is a medicine to apply to illness. When the illness is cured, you no longer need the medicine.

To pass a koan given by a teacher is not so difficult, but to pass a koan given by actual life—that is wonderful! Studying Zen in the sanctuary of a Zen master is like learning to swim in a pool. But to swim in the ocean of life is the koan given by Tathagata. That is the koan we have to pass.

You must get something you can depend upon in this present moment, this present consciousness. This is the gate of Buddhism. There is no other gate. And you must go through this gate. So this story of *Alice in Wonderland* is very interesting. This little Alice, who went through the looking glass—through Buddhism. Alice goes to the tea party of the Mad Hatter, and he makes tea in a cup. Alice says, "Oh, I like it." The Mad Hatter says, "What is IT?" "You know what IT is." I think somehow the author of Alice knows what IT is. Rinzai said, "What is the White Ox on the bare ground?" There is something which is impossible to express, and Rinzai expresses that point with this word.

When you attain bliss, your eyes and mind will suddenly see Buddha's Dharmakaya, not with this eye, but with the "mysterious eye." It is Buddha's wisdom. Everyone has this wisdom. Now I am here, and I know that I am here. Wisdom is very primitive power, it is just "to know." Enlightened wisdom (Prajna) is the power with which we recognize existence. When everything is exactly the same, this wisdom doesn't function with the power of recognition, for there is nothing to recognize. But if something is slightly changed, then this wisdom instantly recognizes that. When you die, this wisdom still exists, it does not decrease. But your physical body decomposes, so this wisdom loses the medium through which it functions. You always have the power to see, but if you lose your eyes, you lose the medium through which this seeing power functions.

Now, why is Prajna so important for Zen students? Because without Prajna we cannot attain *satori*. The word *satori* is not to be found in English. To say "without Prajna we cannot attain *satori*" means that without this wisdom we cannot recognize salvation. If you really understand these two powers, Samadhi and Prajna, your Zen is over.

When you meditate, it means that you discipline and train yourself in the practice of Samadhi. But just meditating doesn't make Zen. You could meditate for a hundred years, but it doesn't make Zen. Samadhi does not truly produce Prajna. Samadhi brings forth this Prajna, which is innate. When you attain the Dharma eye, you will see all the different strata of existence. Although you are in the state of *reality*, you will not be able to see the many stages and phases in the Dharma until you attain this eye. There are people who have felt the great cosmic vibration, but cannot transmit it. Many attain great religious insight, but few can teach how to reach it. They require the higher eye, the eye that observes the law of nature—the Dharma eye. In meditation, we observe the law of mind and analyze mind so as to attain the Dharma eye. Then we can see the other's state of mind and read it.

When you have entered the world of the wisdom eye, you must turn yourself around to see the entire nature of the human being. For instance, you will look at a man and see that he can practice one Buddhist way, but not another; or that he can enter this avenue, but not that one. So according to the nature of each person, the Bodhisattva selects the means by which we can practice to attain enlightenment. Those who have this eye understand all law and can switch their own power to another, so that the other can feel it. Though a Bodhisattva has attained the Dharma eye and understands the Dharma according to Buddhism, his eye does not penetrate the minds of slaves and criminals, of crooked and twisted souls, of the lower sentient beings, or those lost, wandering ones who dwell in hell. The Bodhisattva can only transmit his power to good and natural followers. To reach all sentient beings, one must attain the highest eye, the Buddha eye. When the Bodhisattva attains this eye, it will penetrate everything, even the minds of human beings covered with the beginningless darkness of ignorance and eons of evil karma. The Buddha eye can reach the true heart and the true mind of criminals and slaves, save them from their agony and give them emancipation. The one who has the Buddha eye sees from all sides—sees all the details of the human mind with compassion and sympathy.

The teacher doesn't want to go up the mountain, but if someone comes to him and says, "Take me to the top of the mountain," he will remove his polished shoes and white collar and put on mountain-climbing clothes for the ascent. It is the same with a monk. He may be living a layman's life, but if a novice asks him to lead him to the mountaintop, he says, "All right." Then he may leave his home and shave his head to teach, for many people cannot understand the frank attitude of an enlightened teacher who lives as a layman. This is the goal: Come back from the mountaintop, take tea—"Hello, how do you feel today?" "I feel fine." But no one believes it because this enlightened one hasn't gone to a mountain cave and eaten one grain of rice a day! The Buddha tried this once and concluded, "No, this is not the way." But under the Bodhi tree, he attained! If you can have faith in God without knowing him, you are fortunate. Some can have faith without studying, but our kinky mind doesn't believe it.

You are adhering to the mind in vain, because there is nothing to adhere to. This is the foundation of the Sixth Patriarch's Zen. He throws out all that meaningless meditation and comes back to the original, ordinary, human consciousness. Everybody despises this place, but there is no other place to stay. When your mind is pure and simple, when you are not dreaming, your mind is tense, but pure. When you are thinking nothing at all— perhaps you are sitting on a park bench in Riverside Drive, looking at the Hudson River shining like silver in the rainy evening—all of a sudden you come close to enlightenment. In such a moment realization comes.

When I was young, I went about in Samadhi, but one day I found this place and here I stay. I threw away all those affected attitudes. There are many of them in Buddhism. People think it is wonderful, and many worship such actions. Affected attitudes look wonderful. It looks like a crocodile! I have no tail on my end, no horns on my head. I am a human being on two legs, so finally I decided to live in my present consciousness. After thirty-four years I opened my eyes and accepted this outside, this human world. I did not imitate the young monks; I settled down on my human heart. Some will say, "Sokei-an says that he is a Zen monk, but he is just like an ordinary man." I make no reply, but I know why they think so. Many people go to Japan and see the Zen monks and come back to New York and find me in my apartment, sometimes telling a bad story. But I stay in this present consciousness.

Yes, there is a transcendental world. How can you get into it? There is a way to enter it. If someone should ask me, "Have you entered it?" I would answer, "Yes." If he should ask me, "Are you still in it" I would say, "Well, I haven't come out of it." "Oh, Sokei-an, you are kidding! You are here speaking to me, with your eyeglasses, your nose, your voice. How can you be in the transcendental world?" I cannot explain. I can only tell you that I am in the transcendental world, but you are not in it yet. I am here with you, I can see you, but you fail to see me, the man who is in the transcendental world.

# Cat's Yawn

*F*rom *Cat's Yawn*, published by The First Zen Institute, New York 1947:

### Man Who Is A Sky Dweller

In religion there are three styles: ritualistic sermons, preaching from the altar, and discussion at the dinner table when the priest is invited to a lay house. In addition there is religious discussion among the monks in their own cells whenever this is permitted. I am weary of talking about Buddhism in a formal attitude, as I perform rituals under the candlelights and burn incense in air vibrant with the sound of the gong. Since man is a Buddha, it is majestic and beautiful to discourse upon religion in a rigid, formal attitude. But since a man is also merely a man, and nothing more, he prefers to talk about his own faith in a less formal attitude, or in no attitude at all.

Among our ancient savants, many "disheveled" men attained enlightenment; for instance, Hotei used to sit on the ground outside the villages with a big bag at his side, beating his drum-shaped belly with his hand and laughing loudly. You call him the "Smiling Buddha." Or that famous Buddhist poet Kanzan who lived alone on a mountain peak. It was his wont to come down now and then, carrying a hollow piece of bamboo, and beg for food from the temple. At the temple gate he would laugh loudly. His voice was borne into the kitchen by the rising gale. Jittoku, his friend, would call him and give him food. Without saying "Thank you!" Kanzan would laugh loudly. As he and Jittoku laughed together, Kanzan would depart. But he never forgot to put his verses on a tree trunk, peeling the bark from the tree. Today we enjoy hearing about Kanzan and Jittoku. Both were enlightened monks.

I wish to talk about my faith in a very "disheveled" attitude, just as a cat vomits the breath from its mouth in yawning. In this Western world, Buddhism has been studied for about two hundred years, so I understand. First, it was investigated by Englishmen in Ceylon in order to gain control over the natives. In the second period, this religion was studied by Christians whose purpose was to disparage it in the Orient. In the third period, it was studied as an old Oriental philosophy, and in the present day, in what is its fourth period, Western people are attempting to discover whether there is any element of truth in Buddhism. But in my opinion they have failed. They are merely talking about what Buddhism is, but this "What is Buddhism?" is a great question.

I was initiated into Buddhism when I was still a boy. My age is now threescore years. It was only yesterday that I came to understand what Buddhism is. Let me speak, lying on the floor with my yawning cat at my side, about the Buddhism which is my very self.

To adopt the correct attitude is not to remain silent, because this attitude, this silent attitude, is not silence. I found a phrase invented by an American: "dynamic silence." Dynamic silence is like dynamite, it has tremendous power. The Chinese used a phrase to express this silence—"mute thunder."

The Sutras speak of this profound principle which is the pivot of Buddhism—silence. In Christianity, what is the pivot of their teaching? God. In Buddhism, this silence is the pivot of our teaching. Someone said, "Oh, Sokei-an, don't make that funny face! I can't help but laugh when you do that." I am very sorry, but I don't make any face. I am only sitting here—silence. But there is no other way to express it. In the beginning of my lectures, I always sit thus a little while.

In the beginning, when I was giving you lectures, when I did this, sat in silence, the audience thought, "Reverend has forgotten the word and is sitting thinking about it." But that is not it. There were no words to talk. But some of you said, "Reverend, do you need a dictionary?" No, I don't need a dictionary. This is not written in a dictionary. The human being cannot explain "This!" I said "this," not "this attitude" or "this silence." I said "THIS!" Human beings cannot explain this. In Sanskrit this attitude or state is called *tatha*. Tatha means nothing but "this" or "that." You cannot explain it by words. It is the absolute truth of the state of *reality*. It is undemonstrable; it is unintelligible. The human intellect fails to intellectualize it.

I beg your pardon for my slow speech, but first I must think these things I am going to speak in my mind, then I must translate it into English, and then I must carry out the Dharmakaya itself before your eyes. So naturally I cannot speak as I would read a book. I studied Chinese since I was five with my father. At fifteen, I was well versed in Chinese—in reading! Speaking it is a different matter. I was twenty years old when I went to the monastery. From forty years of age, I began to study English grammar, and ever since I am trying to complete English and translate this. If I really complete English, I would be eighty years old, and there would be no time to do anything! I realize I think too much of myself!

Once a month I will speak of Buddhism in general. The lectures which I am giving now on Saturdays and Wednesdays are a quite advanced theory of Buddhism. Zen is, of course, the eye of Buddhism, the real core of Buddhism. Sometimes they are too difficult for a new audience—so once a month I will speak something that a new audience can understand. Before I came to America, I thought all these philosophical terms—*reality*, *emptiness*, *existence*, etc.—would be familiar to Americans. I was disappointed. At first I thought it was my pronunciation.

A short time ago a group of about forty-five young Christian ministers visited me here. One of them asked me, "On what are you meditating?" "On *emptiness*," I answered. Another asked, "what is the meaning of this *emptiness*?" If it had meaning, it wouldn't be empty. A middle-aged woman minister then said, "Are you wasting your time meditating?" I answered, "If I do anything else I am wasting my time."

A young man who came from India asked me a question: "How do you teach Buddhism in America? You cannot write English and you cannot speak English. How do you teach Buddhism?" My answer was, "I teach Buddhism in silence." I was reproved by my teacher in Japan: "I hear you are saying something. Why don't you keep your mouth shut?" I have not given him my answer yet, but I will—and I will keep my mouth shut. But I must make some preparations before I keep my mouth shut!

Bodhidharma came to China and stayed quiet for nine years. He was selling Great Nothingness. I am, in these lectures, selling my Nothingness. It is the greatest thing that can be bought, spaceless and timeless. Can you hear the sound of one hand? Through that sound you will attain the Great Nothingness. I received it from my teacher, going through many fears, discouragements, and agonies. I am trying to sell you this Nothingness!

I thought I would never repeat the same subject in a lecture, but I have the desire that someone shall carry on this teaching after my death. I must repeat the same subject again and again until you thoroughly understand the important pivots of my way of thinking. In Japan a Zen master does not give this kind of lecture because there are many books written which students can read to gather their knowledge of Buddhism. In this Western Hemisphere I cannot recommend any book which is translated into English by your scholars. Of course there are some translations which were not mistranslated from the original texts, but they always omit the most important pivots which must be emphasized in order to understand what is meant. I shall leave three or four Sutras translated by my own hand, and besides that I shall tell you in what way I am thinking about Buddhism. This will be material on which you can rely to promulgate this teaching. It is, however, very difficult to grasp the pivots of Buddhism.

Isn't it very strange that as long ago as the T'ang dynasty, in eighth-century ancient China, people were crazy to find the "pivot of mind," as today men are crazy to find the pivot of money?

The seventh to tenth centuries were the famous golden period of the T'ang Dynasty, when Chinese civilization reached its highest point. During this epoch, the Zen School of Buddhism swept through China. Chinese history in this period was distinguished by a struggle against fierce invaders, Tartars and Turks, "blue-eyed and purple-bearded," from the west. The spirit of China was strong, warlike, very Zen, influenced by the atmosphere of the times, and characterized by bluntness and force, coarser-grained than today. Buddhism once more took on its original form, its original face—as if the Buddha spoke it directly from his own heart. The Zen masters of China at this time were not reading from moth-eaten Sutras, but spoke Buddhism as it was written in their own hearts, from the innermost man. Buddhism became very clear, but it can be criticized, for they forgot the atmosphere of Buddhism. They grasped the vital point and were satisfied, like the scientist of today who goes to a drug store instead of a restaurant—"Give me vitamin D"— and eats it instead of a meal. If you go to a restaurant, you will have a cocktail, soup, main dish, dessert, then a cigarette and coffee. Real Buddhism must be a full-course meal too. Rinzai gives me a vitamin and I swallow it; it is the essence of Buddhism. The vitamin is only good in theory, but when you eat food that comes from the garden, you also see the farm, chickens, dogs. You must see it all. I wish to show you all of Buddhism, not give you just vitamin D.

In China, where the Zen sect originated, five schools of Zen developed. Rinzai, a Chinese master who lived in the ninth century, was the founder of one of them. No translation of Rinzai's sayings has been made from Chinese until now; this is the first time it has been recorded in English. In Rinzai's time, Buddhism in China had reached the highest point of its metaphysical phase. The Chinese had accepted Buddhism from India with their brains. Now they realized it was a "brainy" Buddhism. It is the same in America. It will probably take five hundred years for Buddhism to reach America's heart. An impasse had been reached from which it was impossible to take another step. Rinzai broke out a new channel through which the slow flow poured into a quick stream.

The Buddhism of Rinzai is different from that of other Buddhists of his time. Rinzai's school has the particular characteristic of being swift and sure—whenever he says a word, it indicates the real point of understanding. He, as a Zen master, did not speak much philosophy. If anyone asks a Zen master, "What is silence?" he gives no answer—he is the answer. The others will say that silence has profound meanings, that if you penetrate into Buddhism, you will enter Nirvana. The Zen method puts you into it. Take it and use it! Do not put a name to it. This is fundamental.

If you examine the words of Rinzai carefully, you will see that he was trying to popularize Buddhism so everyone might understand its true principle, which had become so complicated during the T'ang Dynasty. But today, when we read the record, we feel as if we are climbing a mountain instead of coming down from its top to the town below. Such simplicity is difficult for our minds to understand. I always feel that if someone where to call, "Ah!" perhaps we might find someone in the American far

West or in the deep woods to answer "Hey!" He would not be afraid to look at anything. If in the city you call, "Hey!" they think you are a pickpocket. When I was in the West, I thought America was a natural place for Zen Buddhism. Comparing American students with ours, ours are putting on rouge and white paint and hanging trinkets on themselves.

It was Zen master Baso's shout that made the Rinzai school. Baso made his great shout to indicate his Zen, to show that *reality* is activity. He emphasized the essence of Zen. But I do not shout here because this house would come down! If I gave Rinzai's shout, it would fall down. When Baso shouted, his disciple Hyakujo was deaf for three days. I wish I could hear his shout, so I could be deaf for three thousand years! The Rinzai Zen school does not take a meek attitude. The Zen religion demonstrates the mighty power of the universe. Zen has its own nature. There is no description, no philosophy to talk about. The transmission of shouting and hitting was the primitive method. Today we handle Zen more delicately. Zen has developed. We still shout and strike, but we are not so crude. That was the beginning of Zen. All those expressions were real creations.

These days no one administers such hard blows to the disciple because we are terribly involved with emotionalism. How can we make disciples so? You say business is business. We say truth is truth. To put a disciple into shape, why do we hesitate to use the stick? In Kyoto, the Zen masters are still using the stick, but my teacher and Soyen did not use it. They used cutting words. It is painful, just as painful as accepting one dose of the stick on the back.

This commentary on *The Record of Rinzai* has been long. But

I think three or four more Wednesday lectures will really bring it to an end. After this record, I shall translate *The Record of the Sixth Patriarch*. *The Record of the Sixth Patriarch* is not such a big record. I think it will take about one and a half years to complete. But it was the Sixth Patriarch who really crystallized the Zen teaching. This made it the Zen school. It has been handed down to this generation, and I am now translating it into English from beginning to end.

These lectures I am giving are very important. I am sorry for those who are not here tonight to hear what I may say once in a lifetime. Though it is absurd to try to translate from such a Sutra in this age, I spent all day translating this for a few people who cannot depend upon a poor translation. In the Sixth Patriarch's school he placed all the emphasis on this intrinsic wisdom, Prajna. In five seconds you become aware—"Oh!"—that is the end. So any second while you are working at your desk, or dropping a nickel into the subway—"Oh!"—and it is all over. But we must practice meditation, the foundation of the Zen school. Even though you attain Prajna, without meditation it shines very dim. When you find IT you must be the master of the mind. Yes, meditation is the foundation of the Zen school.

To carry my Buddhism into this country, I find that Buddhism must be applied to Americans quite differently from the way it was applied to the Japanese. How to adapt Buddhism for the American mind is a problem. It is a very interesting problem for the future. I am thinking of doing something in the next issue of *Cat's Yawn*. What is Zen in the American sense? What is Zen to the American mind? It is not meditation!

I think the Sixth Patriarch never dreamed that his record would be explained to Westerners in New York. Reading this

Sutra, I feel that I am in a vale between high mountains and that the ancient simple-minded woodcutters, fishermen, monks and nuns who are living in the mountains have come to the place where they always have their gatherings. I am one of them. From my standpoint as a Zen monk, I am living among mountains in the woods. I seldom meet human beings. Few come to see me. Those are all the pupils living in this mountain. Perhaps they are waterfalls, or shadows, or rainbows, or twigs. There are lions and tigers and winds howling around. We are making a little gathering to read this scripture and enrich our souls.

A gentleman who lived here about six years ago promised me that he would visit the temple of the Sixth Patriarch, which still exists. I thought it was quite dangerous without a guard—but he went to China. The temple is now just a nest of bandits. About ten years ago we gathered some money and sent it to China for the repair of the temple. The report came back that the money had been used, so we did something for the Sixth Patriarch!

After my lectures on the Avatamsaka Sutra I will give a commentary on twenty-five famous Zen koans through twenty-five Saturday evenings. But I will not speak about any answer to these Zen questions. It must be understood between me and you. There is no teacher in the past or present who will speak about the answers in a lecture. This answer is yours. You must obtain it. No one can think the answer for you, as no one can eat food which you eat, with your own mouth. From ancient times, many Zen masters were commenting on the koans. Those commentaries were giving great help to the students. Once in my life I shall give a commentary on a limited number of koans, about twenty-five. There are 1,700 koans, so every student must take a very long time.

In the Zen school, if someone claims to be enlightened, we

say, "Show me." If you do not know, you cannot show. This means to show before my eyes. So when you talk about enlightenment, I say, "Show me." It must be demonstrated. Once, I met someone who—when I said, "Show me"—said, "Look at my nimbus." I said, "I don't see it." He told me, "You're not enlightened." I could have said to him, "I can show you mine." If I gave him a black eye, he would see the light! I went to Boston three times to explain Zen, and finally I succeeded in explaining Zen to Dr. Tupper, president of the Japan Society of Boston. In one word, I said to him, "Zen is: I am from Missouri." "Oh!" said Dr. Tupper. "You have to show me!"

*"It took me 35 years to learn the answers of those questions myself. How can I tell you about them? . . . Zen is as simple and easy to understand as this apple in my hand."*
—The Boston Herald, *February 19, 1936*

When I was in Japan, my teacher lectured on *The Record of Rinzai.* He made a commentary upon every point. He spent four full years on it, and I took notes of every lecture. It was my responsibility to complete it in the form of a book. When I had arranged my notes, my teacher disagreed with the notes. I must confess, a summer day's lecture makes me somewhat sleepy, hence it is very hard to track someone speaking at full speed. I missed many points. Therefore to finish the manuscript, I used my own wits. When my teacher saw this, of course he scratched many lines with his red pen. When the book was published, we offered a copy to the Emperor and Empress. It was received and permission was given to call it a book of the royal command.

When I began to give lectures from *The Record of Rinzai* to an American audience half a year ago, I was expecting to publish it in book form at the close of the lecture series, and I wrote to my teacher asking him to write a preface. His reply was that he would permit me to publish it as a translation of his book, because he thought I was using his commentary which I have mentioned above, though I did not do so. His commentary is far too long. I could not make a small volume from it, and also many of the points in it are impossible to understand by Americans.

When I was young, I came to my teacher, who was himself very young. I had the opportunity to finish my Zen study under one master. He is still living and he still criticizes me. When I translated the Rinzai record and asked him to write a preface, he answered, "What! You? You are too young!" I was fifty then—but I was too young! It is very nice to have someone to criticize harshly, stick needles into one, keep one down. I appreciate this criticism.

April 16, 1939, we celebrate the seventieth birthday of Sokatsu Shaku. During the forty years of his teaching, three thousand men and women had come to study Zen under his direction. Of these he had initiated nine hundred into Zen. Thirteen of the nine hundred had completed the training, but of these thirteen only four had really penetrated to the core of Zen. These four he had ordained as teachers. The eldest of the four is Zuigan Goto. He was originally a Zen monk of the Myoshinji school. The second is Eisan Tatsuta, who is ten years my junior. He is a graduate of the department of zoology at the Imperial University of Tokyo and a professor of zoology. The third, Chikudo Ohasama, graduated from the department of ethics at the Imperial University of Tokyo and completed his studies at Heidelberg. The fourth is myself. Sokatsu Shaku has now retired, leaving his teaching in the hands of Eisan and Chikudo. They are carrying on the work of Ryomokyo-kai, the promulgation of Zen among lay intelligentsia at Ryomo-an and its eight branches in various part of Japan. The seed planted by Kosen has grown to a mature tree, which flourishes under the care of his descendants.

The usual learning is something like vestures. You put them on your mind. Occasionally people tell me, "You don't teach me anything. I am here three months already. You did not teach me anything. You did not answer any questions, and you did not teach me any secret doctrine." It is not a secret doctrine if I can teach it to you. It is secret because you must teach yourself. All knowledge is written in your own soul. I cannot put any secret doctrine on your mind. Take off all those clothes you are wearing on your mind and find the secret doctrine! I teach nothing to you. I ask you to take that stuff off your brain, to take the sawdust out of your mind.

Book? Teacher? Church? You will find nothing there but fragments of knowledge. Truth is not a mosaic, but a spring. It springs out from your heart. That is where to seek it. These lectures are not the real method of Zen. But this is a different world, and I must speak something, swimming out in this unknown ocean.

> I have grown old spending half my life
> reading these books under lamplight.
> September has come and still in summer's garb,
> I wander the country over.

I wrote about nine books in my life, but I am not saving them. I think they are snakeskins. These lectures are also snakeskins . . . but the snake is going. Someday I shall cast this aside—very interesting.

# Your Uncle's Doghouse

## INTERNMENT AT ELLIS ISLAND AND FORT MEADE

New York                                    September 8, 1941

Dear Edna,

The hollowness is hot again these days. How is your poplar tree? Is it standing with tree mind? I am going to move into the new house on 22 Sept. and open temple only for members on 18th Oct. Before my moving will be executed, I shall come down and see you. Do you know "just living" makes a religion. Funny isn't it?

Sincerely,

Sokei-an

ᛉ

October 27, 1941

Dear Edna,

When I do something, I never do anything in terms of good or bad. I am living in the world. I am trying to live. When I do something, I am compelled to do it. There is no alternative. I must do it. If the results were bad, I accept punishment, but if the results are good, I shall accept reward. The result will be ripened according to the time and to the space and to the conditions. If my wisdom were better than others, I would foretell the result. If I failed in my speculation I shall beg your pardon. You know, Edna, there are a few men living by their own understanding. Others are living like shadows.

Yours ever,
Sokei-an

꒰

From your papa
To Sokei-an's girl children:
Panchin, Ivory Leg, and Wagtail
Dear Three Children,

Your papa was scolded by the big ladies for keeping children in his house after the lecture meeting. The ladies said that it was not in good taste of papa and the children, for the human beings do not think it proper. Children, therefore, had better go home after lecture with other big ladies hereafter. Wagtail [Mary Farkas], you had better come some Sunday afternoon for your carving lesson. Papa will come down to see his three children in their own house in the near future. Be good children.

Yours ever,
Papa

February 15 is my birthday. I have reached sixty years in this human life. I have been following the Buddha's teaching from my twentieth year. Of course, besides studying Buddhism, I have lived my entire life as a layman. In the true sense, I am living in a lay house, eating with lay people. I am not living with other monks and not abiding in a temple. Without understanding the Buddha's commandment, I myself would perhaps think that I am not a Buddhist monk, but a layman.

What have I gained by studying Buddhism for forty years? I cannot make an accurate answer immediately. For about twenty years I thought I greatly benefited from Buddhism; then in the last twenty years I have been "ungaining" everything I have learned. In conclusion, I should say I have gained nothing.

I must explain the term which I have used just now—"gain nothing." Its meaning is entirely different from the usual interpretation of the term "gain nothing." If I gain something from Buddhism, I am not following Buddhism. But this "gain nothing" is so wonderful to me!

Someone said Buddhism is like a toothache. When you are attracted by Buddhism, you go to the temple, listen to the monks' lectures, give up your pleasure and time, buy books, bring them home, read them without sleeping, and thus spend your life—ten, fifteen, twenty years—in the end realizing, "I was all right, there was nothing to gain." Well, the toothache is over, and you feel all right. When the tooth is aching, you run amuck, but when the pain is removed, you just smile to yourself. "It is over." I feel just the same. I went through such terrific agony studying this Zen. I lost everything I had, and I gained nothing. I am satisfied.

Gaining something by doing something is an entirely human

problem. This idea of benefit is such a small idea. It is a utilitarian idea that every movement you make you have to gain something by it—go to the Catskills, come back, count money, and say "I gave you ten cents." In this utilitarian age, there must be something to gain from everything. A human being must live outside this idea of "benefit" so he can live on Broadway and make himself comfortable. Doing something all his life, and in the end no one gained anything! A wonderful conclusion to accept and make the basis of human life.

To me, each moment is the last judgment. I am paying back the karma which I committed in the past, and this karma which I am creating will carry me into the future. But I await no future. I accept reward or punishment in this present moment!

The Buddhist mustn't think the mind is intruded into this body. Our mind is living in this great universe. When I walk, I walk with the universe. When I think, I think with the universe. So I think for just sixty years, and after death I don't think? Oh, no. When you think very carefully, this is a great performance, a great drama, for sentient beings. When you see pictures of a Tibetan ceremony, each is a sentient being and makes a wonderful drama. But we are doing it every day. We are in a very difficult period to carry on this teaching. It is like a stand of bamboo covered with snow and bending down. Until the snow melts, it cannot stand straight. It is an interim time of Zen in America. Well, as living things we must go through many seasons. We, however, celebrate the anniversary day of establishing this temple, February 15, 1930.

I was in a hospital. It was a new experience. I enjoyed my hospital days very much. I lost my temper and I had terrible visitors—for two, three hours, all telling their own stories, forgetting me entirely. I pushed the button and called the nurse and threw them out. I came out from the operating room and opened my eyes—"Is it a funeral service here?" My room was covered with flowers! But it wasn't a funeral service. I was still in this world.

In the past ten years in my work, many people have helped me. I feel very sorry that I cannot invite them here. Assisting me and working with me through difficult periods, they were baffled by difficult circumstances. Their hearts were injured and they lost faith in the circumstances, or they could not stay in the group economically. I regret, I weep, I am wounded very deeply, and I worry that there is no opportunity to compensate them. They will be very glad that they have done something, not for the man Mr. Sasaki, but for Buddhism in this country. I am very glad if they have that view. In that view, they will not be disheartened and their service will not be wasted. When I think this, I find a little peace in my heart and my mind.

I am very glad to see you all assembled here tonight, after a long, long vacation. Mrs. Everett designed this hall after a Japanese temple, and she worked by herself to command workmen. Her service to Buddhism is very great. This hall is unique in the United States. I am very grateful to her. I don't doubt that many people are grateful to her. Hereafter, no people dance at night, no one plays the piano, no children shout in the street. In quietude we can enjoy our meeting.

But there is one I will not name who created the circumstances that Mrs. Everett came and picked up and put in a nice place, and there are others whose energy and money have upheld the temple for ten years. Without them this temple would not be here today. I do not call their names, but everyone knows. From next Wednesday I shall open the usual lectures and sanzen. Please come as you were coming to the old temple in West 70th street. We will have some more parties very soon. We don't need to wait for an occasion. I had a hard time making these noisy Americans shut their mouths up. Now the waves of the Pacific are going to rise up, but I feel that I can stay here throughout the wartime.

*Editor's Note:*

*The First Zen Institute of America reopened on 65th Street on December 7, 1941, and from that time on there were two FBI agents twenty-four hours a day. Sokei-an was interviewed many times by the FBI, but the Institute's meetings were permitted to continue until June. On June 15, 1942, Sokei-an gave his last talk, and the next day he was interned until August 15, 1943.*

Ellis Island                         Monday, June 15, 1942
Internee No. ISN-3-31-3643-CI
Yeita Sasaki
Dear Mrs. E.W. Everett,

It was very sudden and there was no time to speak to you. I am here waiting to be called for a hearing. Please inform every friend that I am very sorry I cannot see every one of your faces for awhile. I hope it will be a short time that I have to postpone our meeting. Please keep the cat with you. Wednesday we can receive visitors, but it will be the next week. Anyone who was sponsored could stay in the city, if it were permitted. Of course, when the hearing is done. Please send me by parcel post one shirt, shoes, nightgowns, toilet articles, slippers, and no books. I am going to meditate.

Yours sincerely,
Sokei-an

*⚘*

Ellis Island                                    June 25, 1942
Dear Neil,

The usual environment was all of a sudden deprived of me. I was very much surprised by this phenomenon. I am gazing at the changing phase of it, but it does not enter upon any new aspect yet. Sitting down upon it am I like a sitting Foo dog with a cigarette in mouth.

Always, everyday, which is one and the same day, I get along. In this Bide-a-Wee home there is not many of my own kind of dogs. Please convey my best regards to your wife, and I thank you for lending me your helping hand to pull me out of here. Take much optimistic view, do I not, about it?

Yours sincerely,
Sokei-an

*⚘*

Ellis Island, New York                          June 26, 1942
Dear Mrs. E W Everett,

. . . I haved dreamed of Chaka, golden eyes looking at me from among the weeds in the garden. . . . I sleep well these nights, but I don't look over the sea from the window, for the shadow of the city aches my heart.

Yours,
Sokei-an

*⚘*

Ellis Island, New York                          June 26, 1942
My Dear Mary,

Your doghouse letter amused me. Indeed, I am always in a doghouse from one to another. I have been transferred. I am really a

*Mary Farkas, former editor and
secretary of The First Zen Institute.*

homeless brother and a mendicant. I am afraid that your uncle
might ship me to a faraway doghouse near Helen's country. I wish
to go back to my own doghouse. As for my hope, I confess I pine
for seeing you in that golden pinafore and wagtail. Tell her that
papa missed her.

I am grateful to you for offering me sponsorship. Concerning
that I need only three or four people; I ask of you children, however, wait for me until I come out of your uncle's dog house. If I
were to be detained here for a very long time, you would be the only
one who would come to meet me at the gate of the detention ken-
nel for this oriental dog.

Be good children! And I hope you help the temple!

With love, yours ever,
Sokei-an

⚹

July 2,1942

Dear Mrs. Everett,

The Island is shrouded in drizzling rain. The Avalokitesvara weeps over me today. Here in this fish pond, a fisher of men goes round and round and round all day long. Just now, good news is carried in, and every seventy-year-old fish has been freed from the pond. All the fishes are cheered seeing it go. I made another fish friend here with whom I take tea every night. The anchovies that you have donated to me will be nibbled between this fish friend and myself before we go to bed. I have everything now, but a pack of cigarettes and the holder cleaner. I am waiting for Alice to come from Wonderland.

Yours sincerely,
Yeita

⚹

July 6, 1942

Dear Mrs. E. W. Everett,

My hobby (writing) caused me to be here. This misfortune caused by my pen has involved my real work and makes me die of shame. I pledge my word that I burn my pen. I am afraid that it was too late. If there be luck I may catch the last boat. I think the "hearing" will be held in ten days.

Please tell Mamie that I thank her for her taking care of Chaka's pan. Emma! I am dreaming of coca-cola and pink salmon cut aslant. Pray for me that I may taste them soon. Chaka! *Phmacalo chang golo!* This word is neither Jap nor Chin, but he understands.

Sincerely,
Sokei-an

﹏

July 9, 1942

Dear Mrs. Everett,

When I went back home, my son ran away to a church with his bed. He was the King of my home, and his mother was his servant. Another King has come home. He has evacuated his house. Psychologically analyzing it, I don't think it is a very kind decision to put him against me in the same kind of translation work. My daughter in Santa Anita understands my literary taste, but my son always abhorred it. He has presented my *Nonsense* and that friend of mine (Miss M) has translated it. I was thus put into a pit, perhaps the result of unknown Karma, which I don't wish to repeat again. I don't blame him for his action because he must protect himself. I, however, can give him the advice that his coming to the East is unwelcome. Please write him my opinion about dipping his finger into my translation of the Sutra. It will be too difficult for us.

Yours,

Sokei-an

﹏

July 18, 1942

Dear Miss Kenton,

Miss Alice in Wonderland is visiting me, but I don't know what to do with the other Alice. I am the Hatter taking nominalistic tea with her here in the house through the looking glass. You have sent to me the picnic paraphernalia. I am going to use them with Alice.

I am playing up my fictitious Karma as a fiction writer. I hope this will come to an end soon as a fiction, without producing any fact from it, like the Wonderland of Mr. Carroll.

Yours sincerely,

Sokei-an

August 3, 1942

Dear Eryu [Ruth Everett],

My belt has nine holes. I was using the third hole from the end. These days I am using the seventh hole. I received a postcard from Henry. He wrote on the stone in the picture of Frenchman's Bay: "You must be like this." He thinks that I am a stone while I try not to be. I am going up to the garden.

I continue to convey my thoughts to you. "What is Zen teaching?" The answer is this: "Repose of mind," as Bodhidharma said. Man's busy mind must sometime take a rest. Question: "How to do it?" Answer: "By the practice of meditation." Zen teaching has nothing to do with mental or psychical disease. Zen is not therapeutics. Question: "Why do you practice Zen?" Answer: "Because it gives power to the mind of men who think."

How is Chaka-san? Is he still going over the fence? Regards to you.

Yours,

Yeita

Internee Yeita S. Sasaki          February 11, 1943
Fort George G. Meade, Internment Camp
Dear Mrs. Everett,

. . . The doctor of the infirmary told me last Tuesday morning, after he examined my high blood pressure, that the pressure had decreased a little. I think this improved tendency of my high blood pressure is the result of the practice of my woodcarving, sitting down and concentrating my mind quietly. . . .

The pink salmon, which was the present from Mariquita, was very delicious. It invites a few homeless cats at my camp door at night, for they wish to entertain their sense of smell. I have become very slim. The corduroy pants are too big for me now, but I shall await the day when I will be fat again.

Yours,

Yeita

⚘

Fort George G. Meade Internment Camp    May 20, 1943
Dear Mr. Reber,

The summer has come to Fort Meade. In the evening I sit down upon the weeds. I read books at random till I find myself in twilight's deep; then I take a shower and go to bed. Again, I have something to carve these days. In the daytime, therefore, I take refuge into the work of woodcarving; and it deprives me of the mind tantalized, awaiting for the news of my pending rehearing.

I was so glad to hear, through Ruth, that my son will soon be freed from the relocation center, and that something for him to do was already arranged.

Sokei-an

⚘

Summer 1943

I have some good news. Colonel Hutchings awarded me first prize for my work in the artists' show here. Yes, I am carving again. I have my tools back, and I have permission to take them with me! It is unprecedented—against the law. But there is an exception in my case! The colonel is pleased with his cane, the captain is pleased with his box, and another captain is pleased with his gun. And now

I am carving another gun for the major. But I began late and it is not finished, so I must take the gun with me! Really, the Army has been very kind to me. The major has an Irish Setter and he brought him to visit me, and I carved his face on the gun! My eye is trained for that work. I will make it.

The captain who took Ship's place, and for whom I had carved a gun handle, said to the guard: "Take Mr. Sasaki's baggage and put it over there," and winked at me. Soon Mr. Seki came up and said, "What are your bags doing there? It looks as if you aren't going with us." I said, "I don't know."

All were called up to sign release papers and destination before some lieutenant. When I was signing, I said, "Lieutenant, am I supposed to put down Missoula, Montana?" The lieutenant said, "Yes," and winked.

I had luncheon. Nothing happened. I was so discouraged. Every piece of furniture was gone but the bare bed—even the bedding. Only two little handbags—not even a toothbrush. I lay down on the bare cot. Then another lieutenant knocked on the door, and said, "Come with me!" They picked up Yoshimoto. We were told, "Don't speak to anyone," and were led to the gate. There was an ambulance. We were chucked into it and taken to the bank. They gave me my 155 dollars and Yoshimoto took over five hundred dollars. . . . Then we were taken into another room, and there was everything that was taken away when we arrived. They gave me all my dictionaries!

Then we were taken to the colonel's room. The colonel said: "You are not going to Montana. Are you ready to go where you are going?" "Where are we going?" I asked. "You are going first to Baltimore. Have you got all your baggage? This is a complete secret. Not a word to anyone." Then we were put into a limousine with two immigration officers and were driven off.

✺

September 15, 1943

My Dear Daughter,

I was released on parole. My usual mode of life was restored, and I am living in the residence of Mrs. Everett. I have high blood pressure, but it does not annoy me much except that I have a little headache sometimes. I think my death will not come so soon, and there will be some period of cool October hereafter toward the end of my life.

Write me by-and-by and tell me about the conditions of your life in the relocation center; tell me what you are going to do, what you want to have, and what you do not want to have. I am very poor still and always will be poor. However I am your father. I believe that my love for you will not be very poor.

Your father,

Yeita Sasaki

I have been saved from the jaws of death. You don't know what that camp [Ft. Meade] was like.

# This Life Is Life after Death

You know, when I started to study Buddhism and koans, Zen and Buddhism seemed from my point of view the size of the whole universe. Today, I really confess, Zen and Buddhism are just some old furniture in the corner of my mind. I really enjoy my own mind today, from morning to evening, more than Zen and Buddhism. But this was a gift from Buddhism, so I appreciate the kindness of Buddhism.

This is important. We must have something that is original, natural—which is not Buddhism or Zen, science, religion, or philosophy. It must be natural. I did not find it for a long, long time, and Buddhism and Zen were a hard burden. Now I speak about Buddhism and Zen in lectures, but when I am alone, I do not speak or think Buddhism. I enjoy something that has no name but is quite natural. Perhaps you call it the pure land. It is quite wonderful, the pure land. Someone asked me to go for a vacation to Nyack for one month, but I refused. I just stay here and live in my own pure mind.

When I came to this country and was tramping through the Cascade Mountains, following the Columbia River, I felt the soil of America had the Zen essence. The people's nature is like those great cedar trees in the Cascade Mountains—rather coarse grained, but straight and simple. The wonderful element in the American people is their generosity and bigheartedness, something of the greateartedness of the aboriginal Indian. Tao is already there, but these days human beings have forgotten what religion is. They respond to the taste of food, to luxurious living, to beauty, to the drama. They understand science and philosophy, arguing from morning to evening in terms which have been used for generations. They have forgotten a peculiar love which unites their human nature to great nature. Then art becomes sterile, words become dry, and you are living only for you. Americans live by their personal desire, isolating themselves until their hearts grow cold. That is the shortcoming of individualism. You must accept the other person, and you must accept humanity. When you have done this, your neighbor is yourself, and your neighbor's desire is your desire. This individual you in a democratic country must have heart as a person.

I think of America like this: It could be the meeting ground for the religions of East and West. If the wonderful principle of Tao can be incorporated into the life of America, it will be a different country. Tao is China; Shinto is Japan. What will be the religion of America? This endless continent has rich soil, good climate, fat horses, beautiful women, and smiling corpses! America's advertisements and traditions of "purpose" are of a densely populated Europe. America must drop this old European tradition. In time, in heaven's time, there will come a blending of the Oriental and Occidental standpoints. In this country people will not work from morning to night; there will be an abandonment of the intense purpose so infiltrated throughout. Here Christian love and Chinese Tao can meet!

I came to this country in 1906. In all that time, I failed to find the key that could open both East and West, but now I have finally found this priceless jewel. The religion of Christ is the religion of love. In love, you and I are one. In Zen terms, "I" becomes "Itself" when husband and wife or mother and child are in perfect contact with each other. Buddhism is the religion of wisdom. In the wisdom of non-ego, the person stands a moment, but it supports the whole and is supported by the whole. Without love, wisdom is like a sword, which destroys but cannot create. Without wisdom, love is like a fire, which burns everything but does not give life. Love and wisdom are one thing. When we take this [Sokei-an makes a broad gesture] from the outside into ourselves—it is wisdom; and when we give this from the inside to the outside—it is love. Wisdom is manifested in love; with this love we prove our oneness, and that is wisdom. The two are exactly the same—a marvelous mystery! I have stayed in this country a long time, and I feel I have accomplished my mission by finding this key.

I came here and I am preaching Buddhism. I did not intend it, but my teacher brought me to America when I was young. I studied my ABC's and went back to Japan to remain there. But somehow that Columbia River and those Rocky Mountains stuck in my dreams. Then I was asked to come here and I came. Sometimes I was pulled back to Japan—sometimes to America—like a rubber ball. This is a reciprocal relation. My teacher

*Sokei-an*

came to San Francisco thirty years ago. He stayed four years, bought land at Hayward, and tried to start a community. Then he realized Buddhism could not do anything in America at that period, so he went back. I came to America with him at that time and understood the difficulties. In 1906 it was not possible. Today I find a few friends come to hear of Buddha, but that is all.

We must wait for the time to come. When it does, a little ant will come and raise the stone. It will be so simple. You will realize then. The problems are very great. To give a little office to an egotistic man is a dangerous thing, a very dangerous thing. He will murder your children.

Some day in the future, you will realize that there was some Asiatic Buddhist monk who was giving lectures on *The Record of Rinzai*, the record of a Chinese Zen master. I came too soon to this country. These two civilizations [Japan and America] will meet in the future. Now they are fighting, but the fighting is a sign that there will be some contact later. Physical contact is fighting, but mental contact is exchanging minds. Buddhism came into China after the war between China and Central Asia. Buddhism came into Japan after the war between Korea and Japan. War is always introducing Buddhism to the other country.

When I returned to America the last time in 1928, I began to make a hermitage. Everyone helped me. Everyone fought against invisible enemies. But all those people who helped have left mementos that are still vivid in this temple. Those who will be converted to Zen in the future are our enemies. We are fighting against them to capture them. Many have been wounded and dropped out of the lines, but all those people who have helped have left mementos. Their footprints are everywhere, and their bloodstains are left—I am grateful to them. I love this country. I shall die here, clearing up debris to sow seed. It is not the time for Zen yet, but I am the first of the Zen school to come to New York and bring the teaching. I will not see the end. I am very grateful to you, these friends sitting down here with me, and also to those who are wounded and tired.

I am in New York and I open my Zen school. Sokei-an is not doing this. New York is not doing this. After 2,500 years, from Japan, across seven thousand miles, this is the first time the seed of Buddhism has been transplanted into the soil of the eastern part of America. Who is doing this? Someone will imitate this and open his own temple of Buddhism. Will he, like Rinzai, take the hoe from my hand? If he is in the right climate, season, and circumstances, he will—but he will not be doing it. In religious work, the time, place, and conditions are different from banging a painting on a wall or placing an advertisement. A growing seed is a precious thing.

The seed which I sow shall not die, though everyone has forgotten the monk who was here so many years ago. I followed the Buddhist way honestly about forty years—no one will do it if he is not crazy! I was one of the crazy ones. About forty years and almost now in my coffin! One foot is already in the grave!

Much of the ancient religion of Zen is already dead, but among the dead branches are some living sprouts that I will take out for you. I expect to be here to my last bone. If I should die in Japan, I shall send my bones back parcel post—so please bury them!

I was here ten years—it is like one day. I haven't done anything yet. Every old man rushes, hurries up, because he knows he cannot live a long time. But why hurry? When you are young, hurry! But when there are only three, five years left, why hurry? That Buddhism I don't do—someone else will do it.

Sometimes a monk is living on the top of a mountain. In the springtime and autumn, he carries food up the mountain. But the summer has hot days, and in winter his temple is icebound—he cannot get out. And when he is offered promotion, he refuses it.

These days Japanese monks imitate Christians, trying to do something. But Buddhism is a very different religion from Christianity. This religion grows as it ages. It has many ages, many elements—incarnation, seeds, harvest. The seed reincarnates. It has endurance to meet nature's waiting for something to come.

It is different from a tradesman. The tradesman has an end. But it has no end, just as there is no end to a farmer's life. The tradesman has an end, but Buddhism is not trading—do this and get that! The farmer works one year for nothing; the tradesman sells for profit; but Buddhism has no idea or profit.

So Buddhism is a good religion for a lazy man! The farmer works on the field, doesn't he? And the Buddhist has a great field on which he works—Dharmakaya, consciousness. And just as the farmer cannot change the ground, we cannot change that field.

True religious experience must have time. You sow the seed of a peach or chestnut tree, and it is three years before it bears fruit. You sow the seed of a persimmon and wait eight years. For attaining Buddhist experience, you must wait thirty years—quite a long time. Wise man or idiot, when you enter the way of religion, all must wait about thirty years. You must enter from a true gate, otherwise in thirty years you have nothing.

The outward form consists of the four great elements. Its flesh is Earth; its blood is Water; its heat is Fire; its breath is Air. Flesh will return to Earth, blood will return to Water, heat will return to Fire, and breath will return to Air. You know this quite well, but where will your consciousness return? It is not very clear, is it? Where will your thoughts return? You have thought many things in your lifetime; you study so much. You have a great deal of knowledge. But where will it all go? Will it be annihilated after your death? You must know. You love and you hate. You have many memories. When you die, what will happen to your love and your hatred, your friendship and your memories? What will happen to this everyday life—laughing, crying, smiling, shouting? When you die, will all this come to a destructive end or will it be continued? Living forty, fifty, sixty years, you should not die like a cat or a dog. Absurd! You must know all about it.

The Buddha said, "Those unanswered questions must be answered, as you quench the fire which burns your hair." You cannot wait for the fire to quench itself. "I will wait for a couple of years and it will quench itself." When the fire is burning your hair, it must be put out immediately. The Buddha said, "Your questions must be destroyed immediately. You cannot wait." The people of that day were very honest. People today are different.

Any of you who have unsolved problems about Dharma must question me quickly. For your sake I will destroy the doubt you harbor, so that you can annihilate your delusion. After I am gone, there will be no one to teach you.

It is a very helpless time when the teacher becomes old while the student still has many koans to cover. He comes to the temple through rain or snow and is about to attain the knowledge of Zen in two, three more years of sanzen. All of a sudden he hears the teacher was moved into a hospital. The student doesn't know whether the teacher will come back or not. "I am very sorry for you, my disciples. Please go to some other temple and find a master." Of course, everyone likes the old Zen master; no one likes the young Zen master just hatched out with the smell of the world, the smell of everything. Everyone likes the old Zen monk, seventy, eighty, ninety years old. He was there in the morning; in the evening he goes to the hospital and dies.

It is a great difficulty to find such a man! Once I wrote to a brother in Japan, "After my death, please send someone among your disciples to New York." He wrote back: "There are many heads, but all are solid ivory. Brother Shigetsu better find someone in America!"

Blind faith doesn't amount to much in Buddhism; I must have understanding. I must open the eye of my mind and meet reality. I cannot tell you, "Do this, do that." You must not expect that of any teacher. If you have an idea that if you hang about long enough, Sokei-an will teach you something—you are mistaken. If you are sleeping, I will shout to wake you.

We should attack Buddhism with all the force we have and encourage others to do the same. Its diamondlike strength will prevail: attacks merely clean and polish it. Its power is always available, and if we have confidence in it, it will be apparent to everyone. There will be no need to sell it at all.

I am giving sanzen now from eight to nine o'clock sharp every Monday and Thursday morning. I am getting old now and there is not much time. In Japan, they say, "Get everything out of him before he dies! Beat him up!" I don't care if you beat me up to get it out of me! Do it!

The Dharma was transmitted in three different ways: mythologically, philosophically, and without words, or *reality* itself. The first two are like a rich father who hands his beautiful antique porcelains to posterity with all their pedigree and explanations. But his grandchildren receive only the pedigree; the pottery has disappeared. The third, however, transmits the thing itself, directly, without any names, pedigrees, or explanations. This is the way of Zen—"Here it is! Don't lose it! Thank you very much." The first two ways of transmission are by Sutras and the Vinaya. The third way of transmission is by that written in the eye of Dharma. It is not on paper. It is the law written on your heart. But we do not call it "heart," we call it "eye." The first to receive this koan was Mahakashyapa. The Buddha handed down to Mahakashyapa two things in one: the "pure eye of Dharma" and the "marvelous mind in the state of Nirvana." The pure eye of Dharma is one side, and the marvelous mind in the state of Nirvana is the other. As our hand has two sides, back and palm, so Dharma has these two sides. Mahakashyapa has disappeared from our sight. Where is he now? And where is the Buddha's golden robe? Can you see it? If you cannot see it, you are not Mahakashyapa's disciple. When I ask you what is consciousness, don't shut your eye. Open your eye! Look at me! That is the answer.

You say, "When I die, nothing is left. All becomes nothing. There is neither karma nor reincarnation. My individual life comes to an end with death." This is a one-sided view. In the world of desire your desire remains. When you were living, you wanted to do something—as I wanted Buddhism to be transmitted into America. This desire remains after my death. Every mother and father leaves his or her desire behind after death, and those who join the funeral service, having heard the desire of this dead man, wish to carry on his desire after his death. Someone lives in the dead man's house and enjoys the house if it is beautiful. Someone remembers the dead man's words and thinks of them. Shakyamuni Buddha left Buddhism to us; we are living in it. Christ left Christianity to the world; we are sucking that milk. Every footstep is kept in the invisible world.

> Leave to the earth
> As plants leave the seed
> Leave the dream to the child.
> I am a wanderer
> Having nothing to leave
> But my footmarks.

Do not refrain from burning. Go into the fire and find Nirvana. These were the Buddha's words. People think that in Nirvana all existence will be annihilated and that there will be no incarnation. The Buddha never said that all things must be kept in annihilation. Birth and death is a viewpoint. From the real standpoint, nothing appears and nothing disappears. Birth and death is a subjective conception. Objectively, there is nothing to worry about. There is no birth and death that must cease.

It would be wonderful if we could do it right now, step out of this skin. Shakyamuni Buddha found this way and taught it to us. It is like an orange with one seed in the center. Coming back to the seed, from that centermost place, one can step out because that center is the only spot that speaks aloud about the truth of the universe. Can you find that center in yourself? Where is it? If you try to search it out, it is in vain; if you do not try, it is there like a moon print in the water. If you try to grasp it, you cannot. Do not touch it! If you abandon that attention towards anything, that center is in yourself. You think, you see, hear, touch, taste, conceive, and are conscious of yourself. Where is the center? Everyone says consciousness is the center. Do not make this mistake.

Who knows that your consciousness is reflecting all phenomena? Does consciousness know or does something else know? Something deeper in you knows that the eye reflects. Do not search. The knower is there and you cannot catch it because the knower is the catcher—only the knower knows its knowing! There is nothing more to say about this; all that is left is the practice. Come into that center. I cannot explain deeper than this. I have taught you how to pull the trigger of the gun. Just try it. Step back into that center—only then can you step out.

Practice this meditation. If you see the result of it and think you are now emancipated from your self-existence, come to me. I will prove it. I will tell you if your result truly meets the emancipation of the Buddha!

The Buddha did not discriminate between inside and outside. He thought all life was within him. There is a line in a Sutra that says: "When I look at you, I do not see with my eye: I look directly at your face—there is no threshold between me and you. Therefore you are living within me." Yes, I remember that line.

We study Buddhism to understand our own mind. Our mind is like the ground from which everything grows, but our mind is like ground that is covered with weeds and bushes and trash and snakes and suckers and skunks. When we step into our mind, we don't know where to go. This mind is covered with conceited attitudes, all kinds of attitudes, and we fail to find the true mind. We must cut off all these attitudes to find the true ground of our mind. The Buddha found his true mind long ago, so he no longer needs the method to do this. This is Buddhism. Buddhism is not a religion to get more things from the outside and push them into the mind. Buddhism is the method to find the pure looking glass of your own mind, though it is covered with filth. To become a plain and honest and quite common man, to find you own original mind, this is Buddhism.

You do not need to take any presumptuous or affected attitude. There is no need to take the attitude of a holy man. A holy man is a plain man like everyone. You say to a holy man, "How do you do." He says to you, "How do you do." Your attitude in meeting a saint should be the same as when you meet a criminal. When you meet a saint, you should not smile, and when you meet a criminal, you should not frown. Interview everyone by yourself. You do not need to take any special attitude in accordance with the one with whom you are standing face-to-face. This is the usual attitude of a Zen student. Do not feel you must maintain your dignity or impress your greatness on anyone. Just meet anyone as you would meet the soul of the universe.

In Buddhism there are two gates. One is the Buddhism which is unspeakable—nothing which can be expressed by human words. The other gate is very sweet, like a honeydew melon. Through this we get art, science, philosophy, and drama. If I stand upon the angle of this moment, which we cannot place, I must go away in silence. I shall not speak one word to you. If I take the first gate, I would go away and not speak a word. When I speak to you, I must speak this beautiful hypothesis. This mystery is tangible—I think you will like it when you hear it.

Yesterday was such a rainy day; today is very beautiful, and there was no day between yesterday and today. Sometimes I think this is very strange. Now I think of past and future, and we think the present is an interval, an actuality. But where is this present the past immediately connects with the future?

When you die, you will immediately enter a new life. There is no interval. You will reincarnate into new flesh and there is no moment of interval. The flesh does not necessarily mean "this" flesh, but any flesh that is matter, or the combination of fire, water, earth, or air. All one flesh.

If you ask me what happens after death, I would answer: The soul does not die; it takes on new flesh immediately and there is no moment between "here" and "there." This life, this actual life, is life after death. . . . In Buddhism the soul transmigrates in five ways; the soul will transmigrate into demons, animal, man, deva, or spirit. But all those stages are really here. Here means in this universe, in this city, and wherever you are at this moment. This is life after death. This is delusion, sleeping time. This is transitoriness, like a cloud in the sky. While you are looking, it will change its form. We transmigrate while we are sleeping, from heaven to hell, from man to beast. There is no moment in-between. This spirit has an orientation within itself. It finds a way to connect according to vibration; it goes according to past karma. To the Buddhist, it is difficult to be born as a human being—the sun is in your right hand, the moon is in your left hand, the stars are in your fingertips. When you abandon all forms of nature, you will discover Buddha-nature in yourself. This life is just a dream. When we really awake from this delusion, from this life of transitoriness, we will enter into eternal life and there is no death. We have to enter while we are living.

When I was young, I heard the story about the monk Hoben meeting Bodhidharma, who was holding a scroll in one hand and one sandal in the other, going back to India. When they opened Bodhidharma's coffin, they only found the other sandal! I did not sleep for several nights thinking about this. I asked my teacher, Sokatsu, about it. He said, "You are too young." The next time I asked him, I was forty years old! He said again, "You are too young." Today I think I understand. This is very mysterious. Two hundred years after Bodhidharma's death, Hoben said, "I saw him."

In Shintoism in Japan, during the funeral procession, the dead man's wife and sisters are not permitted to follow the coffin. Always his first son, wearing his costume, with bare feet and using a bamboo cane, leads the procession after the coffin. No woman—queer, but it is an old orthodox Shinto procedure. In these days women, even in Shintoism, are permitted to follow. In my childhood, this was not so. Of course, in Buddhism, all follow the coffin in a funeral procession. In China, they employ "crying men" and "crying women" to wail and mourn; they are professional criers. It makes for a very melancholy procession. In the Zen sect, this wailing to the heavens is not permitted. The monks meditate and say just three syllables: "Ai-ai-ai." No one sheds a tear. This is Zen behavior. It does not mean indifference to death, but that the monks know the meaning of death. They emphasize the profound principle of death.

At the teacher's death, the disciples are not wearing anything special—just their usual clothes, no black or white. The disciples come to the main temple, and before the master's coffin they join their hands, burn incense three times, and meditate. No one speaks a word. Sometimes a layman comes to the temple to offer condolences and raves about the master: "Oh, your master is dead! Such a wonderful man! What can I do?" The monks say nothing as they receive his condolences. If you have a true and honest mind, you cannot say a word in condolence. Silence is the deepest expression. It is a precious time. The master is dead. The man who was laughing and speaking now has gone. He has left a great question to all sentient beings.

### "The Dragon Has Died"

The dragon who was a god
and the guardian of the grain of seven villages has died.
Perhaps it was an omen, one said,
That the harps of the shrine of the god
Were harping a nocturne in the morning breeze!
The folk of all the villages came standing at a distance
To see the dead dragon in awe.
One after another asked,
Had he really died?
Or was he sleeping?
Would he revive?
Behold the dragon who closed his eyes
And hung down from the tallest bough of the tree
Upon the top of the hill.
But his ornamented tail with scales like the rainbow
Was coiled around the foot of the hill!

When I officiate at a funeral service, especially in America, I look at the man in the casket, and I always think, "Indeed, I strove long years for this state of existence called death, and I know what it is." I am not ashamed to lead this dead man's spirit to the place where he has to go. A blind monk, officiating at a funeral service, comes to the dead man, looks at him, but does not know how he lived, where he has gone, or what death is, for a blind monk is just like a beggar. He comes, conducts the service, burns incense, but he knows nothing. There are many like him. And there are many religious teachers who do not know the true meaning of death. Such blind teachers cannot save the soul of a cat! How can they lead the soul of human beings to death? Weeping, bursting into tears, receiving condolences from laymen— this is not the true behavior of the Buddhist.

There was a Zen monk living in a village temple. A rich man who had lost his daughter asked this monk to officiate at her funeral. The monk stood before the coffin and gave a Zen shout, the Rinzai "kwatz!" In the Rinzai school, the monk shouts— that is all. Then the service is over. So, at this funeral, the monk shouted at the dead daughter. The gentleman questioned him: "Where did she go when you shouted at her?" The Zen monk could not give any answer. The gentleman laughed. "You don't know anything about it. You shouted at the dead spirit of my daughter, and you don't know anything about it." Then the gentleman swept his sleeves behind him and went home. Perhaps in the American way of speaking, he kicked the dust with his heel and left. The monk too went back home and that night he ran away from the temple. He was a very conscientious monk. He then went to Kyoto to commence the real study of Zen.

Now after my thirty-five years studying Buddhism there are no questions. When I officiate at the funeral service of a friend, I know what death is, and my heart reaches to his state, but his friends standing by do not know. He has become Buddha, not only enlightened, but has solved his own questions, and that is peace—that is death. It is a good opportunity to meditate and to understand the meaning of death. What will happen after death? What was I before birth? When you see a man who was your good friend eating chop suey last night and this morning he is dead, do you look at his face and say, "I'm sorry?" If you have any sense, you must conceive some conclusion about death.

The shallow-minded man or the deep-minded man will be measured by such a moment.

The shortcoming of Zen today is that students do not think their life itself is Zen. They think that Zen practice is entirely different from the Zen occasion. The T'ang dynasty permitted Zen students to practice Zen at all moments, every occasion—walking, talking, eating—every moment. Zen still exists in such a fashion today, but students and teachers do not show the sharp point of the weapon. We express Zen in daily life in a much subtler way so that the common eye cannot see it. Always in this moment only! There is no other moment for the human soul. If you do not understand this moment, you die! You are not living in your life, in your own nature. You are just eating and sleeping, and your life is not yours. You enjoy somebody else's life. You suffer somebody else's life. You come into life like a dream and go away like a dream. Many are like this.

The Buddha's right view is at this moment, in this place. The Buddha called it the king of all Samadhis. In this state, as a human being, guarded by these five senses and ornamented by this marvelous outside, supported by bottomless consciousness, we are now existing here. Without blinking our eyes, without puzzling in the mind, at this moment we build our spine as a pillar of the body, we cross our legs as a base for this pillar, cross our two hands on our lap—we see everything and hear every sound at once. With penetrative wisdom and tranquil mind we are aware of our own state. We never puzzle, though a million gods appear outside, and we are never lured or tempted, though the shining bottomless consciousness appears behind us. This is our decision at this moment, in this human body, as we are sitting here in the right view. This is the foundation of Buddhism.

This is our faith. Standing on this faith, we enter all directions of human activity.

Before the Buddha's time, they believed that Nirvana was reached only after death. But the Buddha made a shortcut, and you can reach it at once. I began at twenty-three and found Nirvana at forty-seven—a lifetime. The Buddha attained Nirvana and entered it today. Man erroneously thinks Nirvana comes through time. But we can reach Nirvana immediately, at this moment. Don't think horizontally, but perpendicularly. Penetrate with your five senses and find it. If you do not realize in this moment, you will not realize it at the moment of death.

> The universe is endless
> You can go in all directions at once
> Why do you have to go
> wearing your seven-patched robe?

From Edna Kenton's Notes of Sokei-an's Deathbed Sermon:

About half past four, Tuesday afternoon, May 15, 1945, Sokei-an, stricken since the previous Saturday evening, raised himself on his bed, folded his legs, and asked that pillows be placed behind him. Sitting against them almost erect, he asked, "Am I in shape?" Then he began to talk to the three of them, Ruth, Sakiko, and Edna. To his left was a long window overlooking the little garden, and his head was slightly inclined towards it. He said a few words about koans and the work on them. Then in a low, strong voice, very slowly and with long pauses: "You must consider very intensely what you are doing every moment, not depending on any other way. It is the only way. I don't open the window wider; I especially don't close it more. I will open the window exactly as people open it; and I cannot do anything else . . . to one-half or three inches wide.

"I don't open it in any particular way. I only just do it—not higher or lower, standing up or lying down. I do it the everyday way.

"I have never opened it purposely. I just open it as any . . . as any human or sentient being opens it. There is no purpose in opening it; no attitude as to how to open it. I just open it. Therefore, I have no results as I would if I opened the window violently wider and hurt myself. So in opening the window there is no mistake in the attitude of opening it.

"I open it clearly and calmly. I do not look outside or inside. I do not do such things. I open it and I don't commit any error—that is all. It is the real way of opening it, so I don't need to think about my attitude of opening it. My attitude is natural and authentic, and there is nothing to think about it. We don't need to talk about it. So in this normal attitude I have attained something. Therefore, I have to really pay attention to the normal attitude. So how to pay very careful attention to the normal attitude of freedom?"

Sokei-an raised his right hand, first finger: "Is my attitude normal or abnormal? That is all. You might do something and put a meaning on it and that is awfully wrong. I think I have explained this much."

[*Note by Edna Kenton: This part not to be read. Just murmured, not all caught*]

✻

"I see father's face. Why do I see father's face?"

He turned to Sakiko and in doing so turned more towards the window. He spoke of meeting her at the boat when she first came from Japan and laughed with her as he talked of the special "big meeting" at the boat. Then he looked beyond her towards the window.

"And what is that? The window."

"Will you have hot tea?"

"No, I will just stay in the temple."

Sokei-an's talk had lasted about half an hour. There was more talk, and he was given some ice cream. Ruth held Chaka while Sokei-an stroked and petted him for the last time.

Wednesday morning, the sixteenth, at six o'clock, Edna was awakened by Sokei-an's voice calling from the far end of the hall: "I am still living!"

Wednesday evening, sitting beside him, at 7:15, she heard him murmur: "I go . . . I die . . . won't die. . . live forever."

At 7:25 in the faintest clearest whisper, "Good-bye. . . ."

He went the following evening, Thursday the seventeenth of May, at six o'clock.

> I have a window
> Opened for my tea.
> May drifts in from the treetops.
> —Sokei-an

# Zen Glossary

| | |
|---|---|
| *Alaya.* | Basic or "storehouse" consciousness |
| *anja.* | Laborer in the Zen temple who does miscellaneous work for the monks. |
| *Bodhi.* | Awareness or awakenment; the highest wisdom; enlightenment. |
| *Bodhisattva.* | One who is awakened and helps with the enlightenment of others. |
| *Bunraku.* | Japanese puppet theatre. |
| *chakra.* | Centers of energy in the body. |
| *Dharma.* | Buddhist law or teaching. |
| *Dhyana.* | Sanskrit for meditation. |
| *joruri.* | Japanese performance where a singer recites to a samisen accompaniment. |

| | |
|---|---|
| *karma.* | The repercussions of a person's actions that determine their destiny and their next existence; law of cause and effect. |
| *koan.* | A Zen question that novices must contemplate and answer in order to advance in their Zen training. |
| *Mahakashyapa.* | Disciple of Shakyamuni Buddha. |
| *Meiji.* | Period in Japan named after the emperor during 1868 to 1912 in which rapid developments in technology and industrialization modernized the previously feudalistic country. |
| *mudra.* | Sanskrit term that literally means "seal." |
| *Nirmanakaya.* | Body of transformation. One of the three bodies of Buddha. |
| *Nirvana.* | Final enlightenment without remainder. |
| *Osho.* | A personal form of address to a Buddhist teacher or priest. |
| *Prajna.* | Wisdom. |
| *preta.* | Ghosts that fall into a state of hunger through karma because of their avarice, cruelty, miserliness, etc. |
| *Roshi.* | A Zen master. |
| *Rupa.* | Physical appearance, objects that can be identified by one of the five human senses. The first Skandha. |
| *Samadhi.* | Sanskrit term for absorption. In Zen usage, Samadhi indicates the penetration into Zen through intense meditation. |

*Samnbhogakaya.* Body of bliss. One of the three bodies of Buddha.

*samisen.* Japanese stringed instrument.

*Samjna.* Thought. The third Skandha.

*Samskara.* The movement of the mind that is not controlled; seeds of thought, desire, imagination, etc. The fourth Skandha.

*Sangha.* The Buddhist community.

*sanzen.* Private interview with a Zen master where students answer problems that require them to break into Zen and demonstrate it freely.

*sesshin.* A period of intense mediation.

*Skandha.* In Buddhism, The Five Skandhas are the shadows of consciousness that obscure enlightenment.

*Shakyamuni.* The original teacher of Buddhism.

*shastra.* A Buddhist text.

*Shinto.* Japanese religion in which natural forces are deities and the emperor is the descendant of the sun goddess.

*Shunyata.* Emptiness.

*Tao.* Chinese term for "the way."

*Tathagata.* One of the titles of the Buddha, literally meaning "thus come."

*Tokugawa.* Era in Japan that lasted from 1600 to 1868 when the contry was ruled by the Tokugawa shoguns.

| | |
|---|---|
| *Vedana.* | The sense organs; feeling and perception. The second Skandha. |
| *Vijnana.* | Consciousness. The fifth Skandha. |
| *Yama.* | The King of Hell or death. |
| *zazen.* | Sitting meditation. |
| *zendo.* | Meditation hall. |

# Additional Source Materials

—Gary Snyder, *Wind Bell*, Vol. VIII, Nos. 1-2, Fall 1969:
The early line of Rinzai Zen that has come to the West has almost entirely been the work, the karmic sort so to speak, of one man, Kosen Roshi. It was Kosen who opened it up by saying that Western knowledge is valuable and important for us and we must learn about the rest of the world and so started the custom of having his monks go to the university, which was the first time in history this had been done. Kosen also had an interest in establishing a lay transmission of Zen in Japan and so his lineage was open outwardly away from the rather rigid establishment temple Zen; it made them more approachable. And so Soyen Roshi went to America. The First Zen Institute in New York, [Isshu] Miura Roshi, myself, Walter Nowick and his group in Maine, D.T. Suzuki, Senzaki also, all go back to that Kosen line. [Soen] Nakagawa is not in that line but the fact that he was invited to America by Senzaki is the same thing. There is no other line in Japanese Rinzai Zen which has even looked

towards the West.

**—Notes of Ruth Fuller Sasaki:**

Shintaro was brought up in Japan. He'd been in San Francisco. Senzaki kept an eye on Shintaro, and corresponded with him. Senzaki and Sokei-an broke on this. The older daughter came over to look after Shintaro. Married a good-for-nothing boy from a nice family in Seattle. She was in the internment camp with her three children. Sokei-an kept in touch. She came to Little Rock and spent the day. Sokei-an saw his grandchild. Shintaro came to New York in fall 1945. He stayed until February and went to San Francisco.

**—Edna Kenton, "Founding of the Temple":**

In any case, now that Osho was permitted to lecture in New York, Mr. Miya introduced him to Mr. Brown of the Orientalia—then in East 57th St.—and he gave frequent talks in the book shop through 1922-1926. In the summer of 1926, he gave weekly lectures there . . . However, when Mr. Miya was next in Japan, he saw Sokatsu Shaku personally and made inquiries about Shigetsu Sasaki which bore fruit on his return. During this second absence in Japan the final step towards the founding of his temple was taken. On April 8, 1928 The American Committee, which Miya had formed, wrote Sokatsu Shaku asking that he permit his student Shigetsu Sasaki to come to America and teach them.

**—Letter from Elizabeth Sharp to Mary Farkas (January 17, 1967):**

I once insisted on his having a check with a doctor I knew—who planned to take him where there was an electrocardiograph. Sokei-an, through eating a quite ordinary lunch with incredible deliberateness, managed to arrive after office hours to a closed door. He simply did not want to know the facts. It is not strange that he died in the 60s. He had many careers—dancing, woodcarving, acting, swimming. There were poem collections. Also he had a reputation as short story writer and newspaper writer.

—List and comments compiled by the poet Harry Kemp of people who came to Petrillo's Restaurant during WWI and postwar years:

Sasaki, Sokei-an: "The Japanese poet," said Harry. "They all liked him. We missed him when he didn't come—and when he came in late there was a roar. He didn't drink and he had a lot of dignity. He joked and he was witty, but somehow you didn't overstep. If anybody got drunk and did go too far, he didn't do anything you could see, but somehow he stopped it."

Sharp, Elizabeth: Editor, manuscript reader. On staffs of various magazines: *I Confess, Cupid's Diary,* etc. Nice girl—a little bit of a girl.

—Letter from Elizabeth Sharp to Mary Farkas (April 8, 1964):

Now, about SS [Sokei-an]: As copy, I think he might be well nigh incredible—too colorful. In a play, he'd be acceptable as lead character. On stage, all is believable. Sokei-an knew many people in those years. . . . The most interesting of those I did not know was Katherine Ruth Heyman, who lived on the Square, a pianist. He also knew Aleister Crowley, a picturesque Irishman, a patriot. Paul Swan he knew; he was asked to dance with him. Then there was Ito (Michio) on the Square, whom I met. Through me, SS met the Robbinses, Lillian and Todd, great party-givers, on the brink of a divorce, characters who Fitzger-

ald should have written about. This was the period of his friendship with [Maxwell] Bodenheim. M.B. told me, "I never loved
a white man as I did Sasaki." SS told me, "I know a Jewish poet
who puts salt on chop suey." He was not much taken with M.B.
. . . In collaboration they did translations of Li Po that Mar-
garet Anderson ran front page in two successive numbers of *The
Little Review*. SS was highly irritated with M.B.'s overelabora-
tion of the Chinese poet who SS declared was pure like water.

**—Letter from Elizabeth Sharp to Mary Farkas (December 27,
1965):**

No one would recognize the exotic poet, dancer, and writer in
the Zen priest you knew. And few, if any, live today who knew
him then. Among the few things I kept are two photographs of
Sasaki of the Village days. You'll be all but startled at his appearance of youth which lasted until he went to Japan, I think the
last time, and came back with permission to teach Zen. He had
changed into middle age then, whereas before he seemed to have
the secret of perpetual youth.

**—Letter from Elizabeth Sharp to Mary Farkas (January 27,
1963):**

It is a new thought to me that you who knew him so well in
his years as Roshi might not know much about his Village or
youthful phase. Perhaps all his time went to Zen, later. He lived
(I think) on the southeast of the Square—no.72. . . . It was, to
my mind, the age of innocence of the Village. I first met him
when I lived on East 57th Street. On the top floor lived a young
mobile artist, Herndon Smith. He later married Willoughby
Irons, a batik artist. Shigetz (sic) was her discovery. He was
known as a young Japanese poet. . . . At a tea he could indefi-

nitely recite his own poems. He was slender, somewhat taller than the average Japanese. He looked about twelve or fifteen years younger than his age. He was not without guile. All the women talked very freely and easily to him, as to a precious youth. . . . One of the young Japanese "New Women" said Yeita is like a swallow that darts back and forth while advancing, thus slowing his progress always. A keen observation!

In his student days one of his friends said, "Maybe Yeita's account of something that happened is not just as it did happen, but he can make us wish it had happened that way." SS told me he embroidered unimportant happenings, but always told the truth about important matters. . . . To get back to the Village of his period. It was a fruitful, creative period. In that building, number 72, for a short while lived Louise Bryant, John Reed's wife. Also on the top floor, Nicholas Murray, later a top photographer. I once, in the back yard of the Bamboo Garden on MacDougal Street, saw Nicholas Murray fencing with John Barrymore.

—**Letter from Ruth F. Sasaki to Mary Farkas (March 22, 1964):**

Sokei-an had a protuberance at the top of his throat—a knob left by an operation (diphtheria) in childhood to enable him to breathe during an illness. His right arm had been unskillfully set at one time, despite which he had perfect control of it. Highstrung, he had shaky fingers. Yet when he took a paint brush in his hand, the trembling ceased completely. At one time as a young man, he had something the doctors called brain fever. This after the girl he wanted to marry was forced by her family to become the wife of a man who was established and could give her more than a youth with uncertain prospects. He was pronounced dead, but of course was not.

His stepmother saw that he was built for dancing, and he was taught according to tradition, and as a child danced in public. . . . During his Village days he wrote voluminously for the Tokyo newspapers. He also sent short stories regularly to a leading Japanese magazine, the editor of which was a friend of his. He had some volumes of his poetry published. I am surprised that you are still searching through the dust pile of Sokei-an's Greenwich Village days and considering seriously any of the trashy remnants Elizabeth Sharp produces from it. He often spoke of those days in detail to me. There was little creditable and much discreditable in them. As for Miss Sharp, after acknowledging that she was beautiful, the best he could say for her was that she was untrustworthy. Those Greenwich Village days are fifty years in the past. Be careful!

**—Ruth F. Sasaki, Wind Bell, Vol. VIII, Nos. 1-2, Fall 1969:**

Then he went to New York and lived in Greenwich Village and got to know some of the poets of those days. He knew the first of the Beat Poets, shall I say, [Maxwell] Bodenheim, and another person he knew was [Aleister] Crowley. And while his interest in Zen kept on, during this period he was finding out a lot about life. And then in 1919, in the summer, on an awfully, awfully hot day in July . . . something happened to him psychologically and he went straight home to his rooms and packed up his things and got a ticket for Japan and went back to Sokatsu. He also went back to his wife and to his mother and the three children and had apparently a very unhappy time. All the time he was writing and had several books published and was quite a literary figure in Tokyo at that time. He told me he used to make on an average of $200 a month, which was a lot of money in those days, with his articles, because he had an article every month in the Chuokoron, and that was given to his wife.

Sokei-an had a semi-permanent visa for America, which became invalid if he remained out of the country more than two years. He came back to Japan in 1926. Sokei-an had completed his Zen study the time before but this time he hoped he could become a Roshi, which, of course, he eventually did. But before that, while Sokei-an was in Japan, he had one of the greatest shocks of his life. He went one day to Chuokoron and he was told that his day was over, they didn't need anything more, that there were other men coming up who were taking his place and that his vogue was finished. So when Sokei-an went back again, in 1928, to New York, he felt he was completely alone with nothing but his Zen. His teacher had told him that now his life was to be devoted to teaching Zen and no more to earning his living by some other manner and toying with Zen on the side. And so at first Sokei-an didn't know quite what to do. He didn't have any group to go to. He was more or less alone. He had a commission from some magazine or newspaper, I don't know which it was, but not Chuokoron, to write a series of articles on the various foreign people who lived in New York City and made up its population. So instead of going back to Greenwich Village and picking up that type of friend again, he lived for two or three months apiece with an Italian family, a Portuguese family and eventually a Negro family—I don't know how many others—but the Negro family was the last and then he was forced to do something to eat and he went to Mr. Miya, who at the time was one of most important men in the New York office of the Yamanaka Company. Whether he had known him previously, or how he got to know him I don't exactly know, but at any rate Mr. Miya was very interested in Zen, had studied Zen previously, and so he gave Sokei-an $500 and went around and hunted for a place for him to live and to begin to give his lectures.

—Letter from Shaku Sokatsu giving Sokei-an permission to teach in America:

1928

Mr. Jusaburo Iwami and Ladies and Gentlemen:

I am only too happy to grant your request and appoint Shigetsu Koji for this important task of preaching the Gospel of Buddha in the United States. Shigetsu Koji will come to you not only as one of the officials of our Associated Temples, but also in the capacity of Reverend, and assume the responsibilities of opening the American Branch of Ryomo Temple Association, by filling my place and conducting the work of the mission. No effort will be spared on his part in making this undertaking a success . . .

Respectfully yours,

Shaku Sokatsu

President, Ryomo Kyokai

—Mary Farkas, *Zen Notes*, "Inside The First Zen Institute," No. 7, (1974):

For a few months after Sasaki's return from Japan to the U.S. (he arrived in Seattle in August 1928), five men and one woman in New York paid tuition intermittently at the rate of $5 a month into a fund described in a journal labeled the "American Branch, Ryomo Zen Buddhism Institute." William Jusaburo Iwami, who had signed the April 8, 1928 letter to Sokatsu asking that Sasaki be sent to instruct the "many members of our group of faithful adherents of Buddhism," had sent $300 to Sasaki at a Seattle bank operated by a man named Furuya, a Japanese banker, for his expenses. Upon his arrival in New York August 20, 1928, Sasaki went to Iwami's place of business at 621 Broadway, Suite 629, Iwami and Company. "So meager I was surprised," said Sokei-an. Iwami invited him to stay at his home at Dyckman Street. Sasaki agreed to go there. The first meeting of the group, probably September 1, 1928, at Iwami's house, consisted of three persons. These were Daniel A. Cahn, a businessman and theosophist who was working to "get theosophists back . . . to their original Buddhist beginnings"; Robert Sanborn of Los Angeles, a faithful friend from the early Orientalia days; and one more man. The many Buddhist men and women Iwami had described as eager to be instructed did not materialize. A few ("usually about five") young girlfriends of Maude Iwami began to come to meetings. One, named Salome Marchward, lived at 115th Street, where a friend, Fina Perkins, had rented a six-room apartment, which she shared with others. Salome was Iwami's sweetheart. She had introduced Iwami to Fina, and to Audrey Kepner, who roomed with Fina. In the spring of 1929 Sasaki had begun to work at Mogi's furniture repair shop again—on Third Avenue—often at night. Downstairs there was a dining room, where Mrs. Cahn would come in sometimes and have lunch. Meanwhile Iwami had sent a report to Japan, after which Sasaki received a letter from Sokatsu, his teacher, saying he, Sasaki, was no good, had no guts, had done nothing, was a failure—that it had been a big mistake to send him to America. . . .

—Mary Farkas, *Zen Notes*, "Inside The First Zen Institute," No. 9, (November 1981):

While Sokei-an was living at Iwami's, he didn't take a regular job to support himself and send something to his wife. Iwami gave him about $60 for this purpose during his eight-month stay. He went back to Mr. Mogi's carving shop and in May 1929 wrote to the furniture company where he had previously been employed for his old place back or for a letter of recommendation. The Chesterfield letter won him a place with a Mr. Farmer, "who made and repaired many small objects of art." The address may have been Sixth Ave. and 55th Street, which in turn may have occasioned his move to West 53rd Street. I don't have the exact address of where he was living with a black family on West 53rd Street in 1929, but his description of the pleasant large room in the shadow and earshot of the old New York El . . . puzzled me until a few months ago I read a fascinating series of *New Yorker* articles (June and July 1981) by Jervis Anderson on Harlem, which called the West 53rd Street district "the most attractive and most culturally stylish of the black settlements in Manhattan. In the latter part of the nineteenth century this was where the more successful actors and musicians lived or gathered."

—Notes of Edna Kenton:

On May 15, 1931 a certificate of the Buddhist Society of America, Inc. was filed. The incorporation was good, but the name was not. In the first year a woman, Angela Kaufman, came in, prepared to take over Sokei-an, to cast out his group and replace it with her own. She wanted to blot out the West 70th

Street temple and move it to Park Avenue. Sokei-an allowed her lawyers to incorporate his group but against all else he stood firm, and shortly thereafter she withdrew. However, in the trouble and turmoil, his dream of The First Zen Institute of America was snuffed out. His group did not stand with him in this as he had stood for them, and his chosen name was voted down in favor of the colorless conventional "Buddhist Society." He knew of course we could always re-incorporate—but it never came up until near the end. For many big reasons.

Osho sat at a low, comfortable reading table, facing the audience he lectured surrounded by his books, a few pictures, now and then a mandala. There was an unused fireplace on the west wall. On its mantle shelf was a small altar arrangement, where the "pebble stone" was placed first, and that's the image we bowed before. Later, because we accidentally discovered he had wanted it very much, Neil Reber arranged to have a small window cut through the north kitchen wall—"a monk's window" he could slide open and look into the hall when his bell was rung. It was unusual in a New York apartment, and it gave him much amusement to conduct what business he could through it. On the north wall of the lecture room, the living room, hung a framed temple motto, in large, black type: "Those who come are received. Those who go are not pursued." When I went in, in 1933, he had plenty of furniture. Sessue Hayakawa—an old friend in Japan, and acting then in this country—gave him at the beginning a couch bed and a very large Chinese rug. There were some thirty folding chairs, a small competent desk, lamps adapted to his needs, bookcases, and a radio.

He worked over his Zen room—the most precious space to him in his home, embellishing it with brocades, changing its lighting from time to time. His small altar there was very lovely, with its lighted candles, when its mysterious doors were thrown open after sanzen. In that room it was eye-to-eye. Always we celebrated the Buddha's Enlightenment Day in early December, and in February Nirvana Day—on this day too Osho's birthday and the anniversary of the founding of the temple. But of the two it was Enlightenment Day, Sangha Day, that was always the most important. He reminded us always that this day was the day of pilgrimages in the East; every member of the Sangha able to travel came that day to the temple. We had parties through the year. And always we made them ourselves. Sandwiches, cakes, ice creams, wines, were all gifts brought to the Sangha as in the age-old Oriental tradition. "May we have a party next week, Osho?" we would ask. "With ice cream?" he might question, and then: "I offer you always tea and small cakes. If you wish more speak to Mrs. Townsend—or Mrs. Reber—and arrange it. Invite me to your party, please."

**—Samuel Lewis, "Sufi Vision and Initiation: Meetings with Remarkable Beings":**

My first visit to him [Sokei-an] in New York took place in September 1930. Sokei-an had only recently opened his zendo. . . . I remembered having attended nine lecture-meetings and after each talk he permitted just six questions. He never dodged or equivocated, he went straight to the point. . . . If you were an intellectual, you received philosophy, but if you had the Dharma eye you saw . . . you were taken beyond Maya, you entered the realm of the immeasurable. I was fortunate enough to have had a number of private interview and meditations.

Roshi took one into Prajna without destroying the levels between the seemingly finite and the seemingly infinite. Once Roshi was asked if he could see into the future. He answered, "It is too terrible."

—**Letter from Dwight Goddard to Ruth Sasaki (March 1, 1933):**

My Dear Mrs. Everett:

. . . About your coming trip to New York. I wish very much you would meet Rev. Shigetsu Sasaki, 63 West 70th St., N.Y. You ought to know him. In some ways he is autocratic and blunt as the old school Zen masters, but underneath he is true. He has an artist's temperament, is an excellent woodcarver of Buddha images, and earns his money by repairing all kinds of art treasures for Tiffany. When you meet him try and turn the conversation to his artwork and ask to see some of his carvings. I think you will like him, in spite of his bluff assertive exterior.

—**Gary Snyder, *Wind Bell*, Vol. VIII, Nos. 1-2, Fall 1969:**

Shaku Sokatsu was really intent on starting a lay Zen line and Sasaki did not become a priest until after he finished his Zen study. He was always a lay student, and when he said, "Now I wish to become a priest, I want to go back to America as a priest," Shaku Sokatsu was infuriated. He said, "I want this to be a lay transmission," and Sasaki said, "Americans will not pay attention to a lay person." That was his view and he insisted on going ahead and shaving his head and putting on robes and so forth, and functioned as a priest with a priest's name and a priest's style ever after in America and his master never forgave him, never spoke to him again. In fact he officially declared him not to be his disciple.

—Notes of Mary Farkas:

In 1935 Sokei-an decided it was not suitable for a Zen teacher in America to expect to teach Zen unless he had the backing of the orthodox teaching line. Americans would not understand what a Zen koji (lay) teacher could be and had no respect. He could not wear robes or officiate at services. This diminished his possibility of being respected. At one time Sokatsu had as a koan student a Daitoku-ji priest, Awono, who was taking sanzen. Sokei-an got to be good friends and became a priest of Mammanji. Kept up a continuous correspondence. Sokei-an came to this conclusion and discussed it with Awono. Awono took Sokei-an as his temple-disciple and would propose his name—and back him as a priest in the Daitoku-ji line. Awono's temple belongs to the Ryosen-an line. Ruth Fuller Sasaki supposes he gave SA the ordination by mail and SA was ordained by correspondences and [Awono] sent him his robes. His robes were therefore from Awono. Before the ordination took place, SA wrote to Sokatsu, asked his permission. Sokatsu refused and told him to come back at once. That he was not ready, that the inka had been got under false pretenses and wipe him off list. Since a priest must have a temple, he was made the vice-abbot of Jofuku-in. This was destroyed in typhoon and flood three or four years ago. Shortly after ordination, sent wife and third daughter to live in it. SA never saw this temple. Though Sokatsu disowned him, on his 70th birthday (there is a pamphlet on this) Sokatsu gave a talk about his life, said he'd had something like 5000 students for sanzen in 35 years, of those he had given inka to 9. Out of 9 only 4 were heirs, Zen masters—Goto Roshi, SA, Eisan and Ohasma Chikudo. By that statement SA was reinstated.

*Chaka, Sokei-an's cat*

Sokatsu retired in 1937, at the beginning of the war. In Dec. 1941, the Japanese government closed Ryomo-an. When the war ended Ryomo-an opened up. As soon as it opened, Sokatsu order it dissolved. Eisan says, "That is the great koan my teacher left." Sokatsu never gave any reason or anticipation of it. Eisan didn't know what to do. Shortly after members caught breath and 11 out of 14 reorganized and begged him to become their Roshi. The old was left dead. New Ningen Zen. Human Zen.

—Notes of Edna Kenton:

### Chaka The Temple Cat

Chaka was a beautiful but, as to kind, an uncategorized cat. His coat was short-hair, a blue slate gray, with white bib and a long swishing tail. His eyes were bright gold. After the departure of Noodle, a very long cat, of marvelous fecundity—and after a succession of pets including white rats—and with a threat of "two small chickens in the temple—will save purchase of eggs for bacon"—this cat was picked up at a pet shop on the eleventh day of a descending price scale. He had been left there by his owner for sale with ten dollars to provide for his food. He was priced first at $10.00, the next day at $9.00, and so on down. Helen Scott Townsend, one of Osho's earlier students, followed the falling scale—on the 11th day she bought him for fifty cents and carried him down to Osho in a shoe box. This was in early June 1937. He was then half-grown and we calculate his birth date as early fall of 1936.

For several days Chaka wandered about in an unsettled state; then he found Osho's lap and arms and was never lonely again. He would sit in the bay window and watch the trees and the birds in Central Park—as well as the exciting street cats that passed. On lecture nights, at the first move toward departure, he would take a subterranean route, under chairs, to Osho's feet, where he would wait patiently to be picked up, to be held upside down like a soft elongated pillow, stretched out flat with his feet securely grasped by Osho, and to be talked to in the most delightful Oriental gibberish and to purr a contented accompaniment.

Chaka's family tree was often a subject of discreet debate among us. He was a shorthair, definitely not Persian, but with perhaps a touch of that blood. He was more Maltese than anything else, but he wasn't a Maltese cat. After Osho's death, a visiting Englishman identified him on sight: "What a beautiful Siberian gray!" he exclaimed, and pronounced his breed pure.

—Mary Farkas, *Zen Notes*, "Nocturnal Talks" (from several tapes made with Mary Farkas):

When I came to Sokei-an, he would present his face, his original aspect, so you were able to see it, to recognize it; you could develop it. So when you saw him, as he himself described it, people would say, "Sokei-an, why are you putting on that face?" He meant, another person would see him if he were in that state of consciousness and not recognize what he was doing because they didn't have the receptors to recognize it.

He always taught through this absorption. When this happens it awakens something in the other person and they are together in a kind of exchange. This is what he did in sanzen. Sokei-an would show his original face. You can't train to do it. It can be developed by doing it. That's the only way. Crossing that little barrier between catching on that you can do it or catching on suddenly to what it is. Sokei-an said, "When you come to this from another person you experience it, you know that you've made contact and the other person knows it. It is this knowing it that is the point of it." Sokei-an said you can only go so far with an answer in sanzen. Then you must do it [awaken] yourself. It isn't that a master encourages you to do it, but that a person who reaches a level of some real interest makes a demonstration. Sokei-an said, "Self-awakening is the highest teacher." You just open your eyes and there it is. In the first degree with Sokei-an you could get into it, and get into it for a long time. You could speak or do other things and it wouldn't alter it. It was like standing next to a big gong and feeling its vibration go all through you. But it was more than that. It's as if you had an electric light you could switch on in a room. You could put it on and the room would be instantly full of light—

your eyes would be open and you would see into the brightly lighted room. Every night Sokei-an would come in, and he would immediately present himself to us, and we would be there, if we were with it, he would be there, too. So there was no gradual coming into it. We would be in it. We don't teach Zen. We recognize it and say "that is it."

*Editors note:*

*The mind-to-mind contact Mary experienced so vividly with Sokei-an is explained by Sokei-an in the "Awakening Is My Teacher" chapter—where I have included his commentaries on the Sixth Patriarch's effulgence, Rinzai's talk on the seal of mind and revealing the fiery brand, and the koan of Mahakashyapa's golden robe—trying to explain this powerful shared experience that is revealed when all is peeled away in deepest Samadhi. It is the naked mindflow knowing itself. Both as an editor and as someone who played with Mary in "this," I felt I had to give interested readers a few clues, but as Sokei-an said, "I shall explain, but if you cannot understand, do not blame me. . . . In my temple the transmission is from my mind to your mind and the seal is in the form of my Buddha Mind, and I am proving your attainment. . . . There is no such transmission without looking at each other. It can only be done face-to-face, eye-to-eye. This eye I am talking about is a very important part of Buddhism. This eye is the physical eye, the deva eye, the eye of wisdom, the eye of Dharma, and the eye of Buddha. In Buddhism, all theories take this hairpin turn. The physical eye and the Buddha eye are the same."*

*For Sokei-an, hibernating in meditation was not Zen, sanzen was not Zen, and lectures were not Zen. You must break into*

*Zen in your everyday life, express this profound Samadhi, and in the ever-changing circumstances before your eyes, manifest the lightning-fast intuition of wisdom in action. It is the way Zen students recognize each other. The wonderful part of it all was both Sokei-an and Mary always loved to say it was "nonsense" without purpose or meaning.*

—From Sokei-an's first pamphlet for the Buddhist Society at 63 West 70th Street (early 1930s):

"Contrive not a word to explain to explain the Dharma.
Pointing out his original nature directly,
Make him a Buddha."

—Undated note by Edna Kenton:

Not long before this evening, during some tea hour, I had spoken of *Alice in Wonderland*, which Osho [Sokei-an] had never read or heard of. We talked a little of Lewis Carroll, a professor of mathematics; I suggested that this was perhaps a child's tale of three-dimensional matter in fourth dimensional space! Lindley Hubbell offered his copy to Osho and brought it up the following lecture night. Osho read it with delight; said he never had dreamed there was in English such good 'nonsense' and began to refer to it in his lectures—"That little Alice in her Wonderland," "That little Alice in her mirror!"

—Review of *Cat's Yawn* by Aldous Huxley:

". . . It is to be hoped that the present reissue of *Cat's Yawn* will startle or delight some of its Western readers into taking the step that leads from mere nature mysticism or mere existentialism, to an actual trial of those expedient means to man's Final End, which long experience has proved to be effective."

—Review of *Cat's Yawn* by Alan Watts:

"*Cat's Yawn* is a collection of material of the greatest value. Sokei-an's editiorial articles show the deepest insight, and we should be grateful to The First Zen Institute of America for making available for the first time the writings of one who is without a doubt among the greatest exponents of Zen in our time."

—Rick Fields, "How the Swans Came to the Lake":

Mary Farkas: "Sokei-an played not only the human roles . . . but could be a golden mountain or a lonely coyote on the plains. At other times a willowy Chinese princess or Japanese Geisha would appear before our eyes. . . . There was something of the Kabuki's Joruri, something of the Noh's otherworldliness, something of a fairy story for children, something of archaic Japan. Yet all was as universal as a baby's first waaah."

—Letter from Ruth Sasaki to Edna Kenton (June 14, 1944):

Dear Edna,

. . . [Osho's] ability to do continued work is improving also. He has just about finished his going over of the Rinzai. He will finish before he leaves for home. Which means that when he gets settled he can begin again on the commentary. He is getting somewhat bored now, another good sign, of course, and looks forward to beginning giving sanzen, saying he is going to have it every day from now on. . . . I wonder if Chaka will want to come home. I am certainly not going to get up at six thirty to feed him. I draw the line there. But I am glad that others have found out through living with him that Chaka is NOT a cat. Osho and I both send our love, to all of you.

Sincerely,

Ruth

—Letter from Byard Williams M.D. to Ruth Sasaki (March 10, 1945):

Dear Mrs. Sasaki,

This is to confirm our conversation about your husband, Mr. Yeita S. Sasaki. He has had high blood-pressure for many years and is showing now a great deal of evidence of permanent damage to his cardio-renal-vascular apparatus. He has had a stroke and definite coronary occlusions in the past, which, of course, are further evidences of the damage to his blood-vessels.

Recently he has been showing increasing severe headaches and palpitations. His blood-pressure when I took it was 276/150. This condition of rise in blood-pressure, headaches and so on, is of grave prognostic significance and, at this time, any worry or any strain, mental or physical, could well precipitate another stroke, or possibly, another coronary occlusion. I feel, therefore, that it is imperative for the sake of his health and life that he be completely freed of all worries and anxieties, even one so relatively minor as that of filling out a form for release from parole, with the attending anxiety of waiting for official action on the appeal. I do hope it will be possible to give Mr. Sasaki this complete rest and freedom, as with it he can hope for a further period of comfortable and useful life.

—Letter from Edna Kenton to Fina Perkins (July 10, 1945):

"That woman" [Ruth Everett, later Ruth Sasaki] as you call her, and for a long time she fully deserved the title, took over in 1939— Audrey [Kepner] had left in early 1938. Osho talked very seriously to a few of us, asking us for once in his lifetime to accept his handling of a situation without interference. It was a situation. She made every mistake possible to make in a group, but I always had more faith than most in Osho's long-range wisdom. I knew that he never did anything apart from his safeguarding of Zen. He foresaw the dark days to come, but it was very difficult for a while.

In September 1941, he moved from West 70th to 124 East 65th, to a nice old house purchased the preceding May, remodeled for a Shrine Room, etc. He lectured there through November. On December 6th there was a housewarming party and a gift of $1,000.00 from a Buffalo woman. The next day came Pearl Harbor; temporary closing of lectures, never again to be given to the public; routine investigation by FBI and long waiting. On June 15, 1942, he was taken to Ellis Island. On September 11th he had a hearing; on October 2nd he was sent to Fort Meade. His internment was perhaps a foregone conclusion at that time; but nothing can ever excuse the ineptitude with which that hearing was handled. Its single good is that it began to change Ruth from a woman sure she could handle anything into a creature shocked and dismayed, realizing for the first time that Osho's group, and no one individual, was his strength.

**—Ruth Sasaki, Wind Bell, Vol. VIII, Nos. 1-2, Fall 1969:**

We opened the Institute there (65th Street) on the 7th of December, 1941, and from that time on there were two FBI people under the present apartment 24 hours a day. Mr. Sasaki was interviewed many times by the FBI and so was I, but the meetings were permitted to continue until June. On the 15th of June, 1942, he gave his last talk and the next day he was interned until August 15, 1943.

**—Character witnesses on behalf of Mr. Yeita S. Sasaki regarding Sokei-an's internment (1943):**

Mrs. Edward Warren Everett, Lt. Comdr. George B. Fowler, USNR, Mr. Lindley Hubell, Mr. Jun Iwamatsu, Mr. Y. Mogi, Dr. R. Stirling Mueller, Rev. Henry Platov, Mrs. Helen Scott Townsend,

Rev. Alan Wilson Watts.

**—Postcard from Edna Kenton to Helen Townsend (January 1950):**

... I shall be much surprised if her mission (i.e. Ruth Sasaki's trip to Japan to find a new Zen master for the Institute) there has succeeded in any way as she planned. Osho said enough to me during these last months to make me feel that succession comes with time and circumstances that appear proper there rather than here. Of course war with the West destroyed many precedents—no one knows. There are many ways of seeking—whether this way is the right way I do not know. This postcard is in essence a series of I Do Not Knows many times repeated. I do know this. Osho looked forward a century. He didn't count by decades, for his work here to bear fruit.

# Sources

## SOKEI-AN'S PUBLISHED WORKS

*Amerika yawa* (Night Talks about America). Tokyo: n.p., 1922.

*Ananda and Mahakasyapa.* New York: n.p., 1931.

*Beikoku o hôrô shite* (Vagabond in America). Tokyo: n.p., 1921.

*Cat's Yawn.* New York: The First Zen Institute, 1940-41.

*Doru no nyoninzô* (Portrait of the Dollar Woman). Tokyo: n.p., 1928.

*Hentai magaikô* (Thoughts on the Red-Light District). Tokyo: n.p., 1928.

*Jonan bunka no kuni kara* (From the Land Troubled by Women). Tokyo: n.p., 1927.

*Kane to onna kara mita Beikoku oyobi Beikokujin* (America and Americans Seen from the View of Money and Women). Tokyo: n.p., 1921.

*Kyôshû* (Homesickness [poetry collection]). Tokyo: n.p., 1918.

*Zen Eye: A Collection of Zen Talks.* Mary Farkas, ed. New York: Weatherhill, 1993.

*Zen Pivots: Lectures on Buddhism and Zen.* Mary Farkas and Robert Lopez, eds. New York: Weatherhill, 2000.

Sokei-an was also a regular contributor to the following publications: *Chûô koron*, the *Japanese-American Times of New York*, and the *Great Northern Daily News* (Seattle).

## IN PREPARATION FOR PUBLICATION

Mary Farkas, Robert Lopez and Peter Haskel, eds. "Original Nature: Zen Comments on the Sixth Patriarch's Platform Sutra," *Zen Notes.* New York: The First Zen Institute, n.d.

Robert Lopez, ed. "The Record of Rinzai."

## SOURCES

Omuro Akira. *Sasaki Shigetsu hiwa* (A Hidden Story of Sasaki Shigetsu). N.p., 1976.

Mary Farkas, George Fowler, and Edna Kenton. Koan Books.

Mary Farkas and Ruth Sasaki. Unpublished Notes.

Rick Fields. *How The Swans Came to the Lake.* Boulder: Shambala Publications, 1981.

Informal Case Record of Yeita Sokei-an Sasaki from Peal Harbor until his Internment at Fort George G. Meade, MD.

Iohara Junichi. "What I Remember about Sokei-an."

Edna Kenton. "Autobiographical Reminisces by Sokei-an as told to Edna Kenton in 1945."

Edna Kenton. Diary of Edna Kenton during Sokei-an's Internment.

Edna Kenton. "Founding of the Temple." The First Zen Institute Archives, 1949.

*Kyomo.* New York: The Buddha Mind Society, 1928.

Samuel L. Lewis. *Sufi Vision and Initiation: Meetings with Remarkable Beings.* San Francisco: Sufi Islamia/Prophecy Publications, 1986.

Letters of Elizabeth Sharp, Alan Watts, Robert Sanborn, James Pratt, Edna Kenton, Dwight Goddard, Sokei-an Sasaki, Sakiko, George Fowler, Mary Farkas, and Ruth Sasaki. The First Zen Institute Archives.

Ruth F. Sasaki. Memorandums A, B, C, and D on Sokei-an Prepared by Ruth F. Sasaki for the FBI.

Sokei-an Sasaki. "A Skeletal Biography." The First Zen Institute Archives.

Sokei-an Sasaki. Untitled Collection of Sokei-an's English Poems, Short Stories and Fairy Tales.

Tea Talks: Informal Conversations in The First Zen Institute Archives. The First Zen Institute Archives.

Kubota Utsubo. "A Man Called Shigetsu."

Alan Watts. *In My Own Way.* New York: Random House, 1974.

*Wind Bell* 8, nos. 1-2 (Fall 1969).

*Zen Notes 1954-2003.* New York: The First Zen Institute, 1954-2003.

## ROUGH SURVEY OF SOKEI-AN'S LECTURES AND TRANSLATIONS

*Agamas*: Translated text and commentary. First Series: Primitive Buddhism. Approximately forty-five lectures from September 1, 1934 to July 20, 1935. Second Series: ten lectures on Sunday mornings from April 4, 1936 to June 20, 1936. Third Series: ten lectures on Sunday mornings from January 9, 1938 to March 13, 1938. Fourth Series: forty-seven lectures on Saturday evenings from June 10, 1939 to June 22, 1940. Fifth Series: ten lectures on Saturday evenings from April 11, 1942 to June 13, 1942.

*The Five Measures (Gokyoshikwan)*: Translated text and commentary. Sixty-seven lectures on Saturday evenings from December 4, 1937 to August 1, 1938.

*Buddhist Terms*: First Series: ten lectures on Saturday evenings from June 16, 1934 to August 25, 1934. Second Series (also called "Terms of Dharma"): twelve lectures on Saturday evenings from January 5, 1936 to March 28, 1936. Third Series: twenty-three lectures on Sunday mornings from January 31, 1939 to June 18, 1939.

*Commentary on Warren's Translation of the Mahaparanirvana Sutra*: Eight lectures on Sunday mornings from March 20, 1938 to April 24, 1938.

*Maharaja Sutra*: Slight translation of text and commentary (unfinished). Seven lectures on Sunday mornings from November 13, 1938 to

January 8, 1939.

*Mahayana Buddhism*: First Series: twenty-one lectures on Saturday evenings from August 3, 1935 to December 28, 1935. Second Series: four lectures on Saturday evenings from June 27, 1936 to July 25, 1936.

*Miscellaneous Lectures*: First Series: twenty-five lectures on Sunday mornings from May 1, 1938 to November 6, 1938. Second Series: seven informal lectures on Wednesday and Saturday evenings from November 13, 1940 to December 4, 1940. Third Series: five informal lectures on Wednesday and Saturday evenings from March 4, 1941 to March 19, 1941. Fourth Series: twenty-one lectures on Saturday evenings from November 8, 1941 to April 24, 1942.

*Outline of Buddhism*: First Series: fourteen lectures on Sunday mornings from October 3, 1937 to January 2, 1938. Second Series (also called "Summary of Buddhism"—lectures and some translation of the Mahaparanirvana Sutra): thirty-nine lectures on Saturday evenings from July 3, 1940 to July 19, 1941.

*The Record of Rinzai*: Translated text and commentary. First Series: 167 lectures on Wednesday evenings from April 20, 1932 to July 24, 1935. Second Series: twenty-seven lectures on Wednesday evenings from November 12, 1941 to June 10, 1942.

*The Sixth Patriarch's Sutra*: One hundred ninety lectures given on Wednesday evenings from July 31, 1935 to June 7, 1939.

*Sutra of Perfect Awakening*: Translated text and commentary. One hundred twenty-one lectures given on Saturday and then Wednesday evenings from July 2, 1938 to July 23, 1941.

*Twenty-five Koans*: Translated text and commentary. Twenty-five lectures on Saturday evenings from January 8, 1938 to June 25, 1938.

# Acknowledgments

*I* would like to thank the following: all of Sokei-an's students who took notes, saved letters, wrote down their recollections, and gave their support; Edna Kenton, Institute historian and archivist; Mary Farkas, secretary of the Institute, collator of Sokei-an's lectures and biographer; and Bob Lopez for help with the original sources and his continuing work with Peter Haskel seeing Sokei-an's translations and teachings into print. I am particularly grateful to Peter Haskel, Zen scholar, First Zen Institute resident, and friend, for the patient editing of drafts and for the laughter and encouragement. I would like to thank John Storm, vice president of the Institute, for his help editing the introduction. I also wish to acknowledge Peeter Lamp, current editor of *Zen Notes*, friend and First Zen Institute resident, for his help with transcribing of the first draft and his work organizing the photo layout. All photographs courtesy of The First Zen Institute of America.